A Determined Hope

~ Jeanie Williams ~

A Determined Hope

My Journey to
True Health and Freedom

The power of faith can do endless wonderful things in a person's life. The life of Jeanie Williams is a great example of that. In *A Determined Hope*, Jeanie shares her life story about walking through adversity and triumph to find God's love and peace at the other end. With her husband Lee at her side, Jeanie has spent her life, much as Jesus did, in service to others. Her remarkable story of faith is inspiring and heartfelt. I have read her story several times and find more value in it every time I sit down with it.

—MIKE QUAYLE

Jeanie's story is woven with both respect and honesty. She allows an entrance into the personal and financial difficulties, the storms, the struggles, the depression, and the health calamities. We all stood beside her as she worked through the painful journey with many bright and happy moments interspersed. And all the way along she points to Jesus with Scriptures at just the right moments to impact the truth that He is her solid grounding through life. This book is wrapped up with joy and fullness and blessing that brings us to a solid assurance that God is able to work all things together for good.

—MARY ANN ENNS

I love this book!!! The book is truly an inspiration to anyone who will read it. So glad you are sharing your faith with the rest of us.
—SHAROL ANDERSON

Wow! God has worked tremendously through Jeanie and Lee's lives! I LOVED the book! Jeanie pours her heart out, being transparent and open about her life! My heart is so moved by Jeanie's compassion to share her life with others.
—SHERRY GERLOCK

Absolutely wonderful. Shed a few tears. Jeanie's story is such an inspiration to many people.
—PAM AUERBACH

A Determined Hope: My Journey to True Health and Freedom
Copyright © 2022 by Jeanie Williams

Written with the help of Mindy Hirst, Generous Mind, LLC. Edited by Ellen Rasmussen.

Hardcover:
ISBN: 979-8-218-08798-2

Kindle:
ISBN: 979-8-218-08799-9

Cover design and typeset by www.greatwriting.org

At the cabin

Dedication
This book is dedicated to our children; Chad, Heather and
Brent and our grandchildren.
Josiah
Vanessa
Tiffany
Kayla
Caleb
Justin
Heidi
Tyler
Michael
Ethan
Tessa
Austin
Tyrell
Katrina

Prologue

"So good to see you! Come on in! Glad you're here!"

I usually welcome visitors at the cabin door and ask if I can make them some tea. If you came to my door, I would offer you something to eat and make sure you had everything you needed. Then, if the weather is good, I might invite you to sit outside on the porch where we could chat. If the wind is howling like it often does in Iowa, we might instead sit by the wood burning stove or at the kitchen table.

Today I cannot open the literal door for you. Instead, you had to open this cover, and as you read, you will have to imagine my joy at seeing you come up the rocky drive.

This is the story of the journey that I've been on with Jesus and his faithfulness in guiding me through many health, family, and career challenges. I hope that as you consider my story, you will begin to look at your own journey. Maybe you will see where you have you picked up unhelpful ideas and consider asking God to renew your mind in those areas.

If Jesus hasn't been with you on your journey so far, my hope is that you will consider asking him to meet you on your path right where you are so he can guide you toward hope and health.

My hope and prayer for you is for good health, joy, hope, nurturing, and growth. I hope that through these reflections you will be encouraged along your path.

Jeanie,

Part One, God Prepares

1

Learning to Walk

*And I am certain that God, who began the good work within
you, will continue his work until it is finally finished on the
day when Christ Jesus returns.*
Philippians 1:6 (NLT)

A squirmy little face moved in the crook of my arm. It
was both new and familiar. Josiah, our first grandchild,
was safe and warm with me on the couch in his parents'
new little apartment. I could feel the strength in my arms as
I held his weight firmly against me. My stomach fluttered a
bit. Could this be happening? I looked around at my son and
daughter-in-law, tired and happy. I looked at Lee, my husband, and then at the baby's little round head and searched
for matching features. Family. Such a mystery and a blessing.

A flood of relief and thankfulness filled my heart in this
moment as a memory crept from the back of my mind—a
perturbing thought that had bothered me for two years,
"Would I ever be able to hold my grandbabies?"

I tried to shake the thoughts away, but the memories

crowded in. I heard the doctor's voice telling us my diagnosis of multiple sclerosis two years earlier. I remembered the MS patients I had cared for as a nurse, and their decline, which ended in nursing homes and wheelchairs. I remembered the fear at hearing I had the disease and the hot tears that Lee and I cried in the car on the way home from the appointment. And then I remembered the fretting. So much fretting at what I may or may not experience.

My whole life had been filled with being busy and meeting high expectations. I liked to be on the move, accomplishing things. Helping people as a nurse, running an efficient home, and being available to people was what I knew and was comfortable with. When the doctor told me about the MS, I wondered how I was going to fight a disease that would directly attack my ability to perform. I couldn't imagine a life of stillness and pain, depending on others for the things I needed. I wanted to be the one to care for others, not the other way around.

But here I was holding Josiah as he started his own life journey. My fear of not holding my grandchildren had not come true and I was filled to the brim with gratitude at not missing this moment. Not only that, but now I was coming to the point where I could face my MS without as much fear or worry. How was this possible? What was happening within me? Or a better question; not *what* was happening, but *who*?

God was happening. He was changing and remaking me.

On Being Made

Before any of us are remade, we are made. Just like little Josiah was made in his mom and was now embarking on a journey to acquire values and beliefs to help him in his life walk; I had been on my journey picking up beliefs and values along my path that helped me in mine.

On my journey, I had to learn to walk, stretch, jump,

dart, hike, bend and run. My body, mind and spirit grew as I walked along the path in front of me, making decisions on whether to go one way or another. Sometimes I had to decide what to do when I found a tree in the road or a baby bird that fell out of its nest.

I also picked up values and beliefs along the road that were not helpful to me. Like pebbles, I tucked them into my pockets thinking they would help me. Some of these beliefs and values were false or unhelpful. Many of the beliefs were not based in truth and so had the effect of weighing me down and making my journey harder. Some of the values caused my priorities to be out of order and so got in the way of more important things.

These are the things that God would need to remake in me, but first I had to be made.

I loved choring with my daddy.

15

Walking the Circle

· · · · · · · · · · · · · · · · ·

When God put me together, he placed me on a South Dakota farm with a mom who had dreamt of being a nurse someday and a dad who was a successful farmer. It was on this farm with these special people that my life path began.

My early movements were around the circle of home, school, and the little country church we attended three times a week. I was a busy little girl. Whether I was running around the house with the dog, walking the farm with Dad on his chores, playing games in the school yard, or giggling with friends at church, I was on the move. Each gallop, step and hop moved me farther down the path of learning the things God would use later in my life.

Expectations were high at home. We worked, and we worked hard. Mom said, "You don't sit down until the work is done," and the work was never done. As early as I can remember, work was important to me.

I learned how to work hard and really pour myself into the jobs I was doing. But the work wasn't all bad. Yes, I was scared as I carefully gathered the eggs under the old setting hens. Often, they pecked my hand, which hurt! But there were nights when the weather turned cold, and Daddy said we needed to bring the baby calves into the house to keep them warm through the night. Oh, how I loved to feed them bottles of milk and have their soft sounds in the dark to keep us company.

It was wonderful to work with my dad and help him with the cows, sometimes in the barn or in the pasture, feeding and haying them. I especially loved those baby calves! They were so cute with their pure white faces and soft warm reddish-brown hair. It felt so motherly to let them suckle my fingers. When Dad and I returned them to their mothers in the barn lot, they would run and jump with such energy.

And sometimes we stopped working and played. Dad

I loved being a girl and dressing up!

would pull me on my snow saucer dish behind his pick-up around the yard and barn. It was such fun for me. However, when I was in the eighth grade, I fell off the dish and hit my head hard. I remember coming into the house and mom asking me a couple of simple questions that I couldn't answer. They rushed me to the hospital where they found I had a slight concussion. Dad and Mom were so concerned. Maybe that explains why I am the way I am!

I often had to play by myself because we lived on a farm far from town. There weren't kids close by that I could play with, and my big sisters (12 and 20 years older than me) were busy doing grown-up things. I was used to keeping myself company and occupied, but even as early as four years old, my imaginary play involved caring for people—even if I had to make up the people myself!

One of my favorite games to play on my own was my imaginary restaurant that served the most delicious mud pies. My invisible customers smiled as I passed out hand-made menus. I studied my mud recipes closely as I prepared the delights I served. Serving even imaginary people gave me so much joy.

Over and over, I read a Little Golden Book about a small girl, *Nurse Nancy* and was mesmerized by how she fixed people's injuries and made them better. I wanted to be like that little girl and take people's pain away.

Growing up I felt valued. My parents loved me very much, and with the age gap between us sisters, I got a lot of attention. Dad took the time to drive me to the country school and pick me up. It was a two-mile drive the first four years to South Buffalo, first through fourth grade; and four miles to North Buffalo, fifth through eighth grade.

Mom and I often had to walk the road of grace with my dad. Dad always had a big smile and was so kind and fun to be around when sober. But when the crops needed to come in and days got too long, he would go out with a buddy and drink too much. When he came home, he wasn't the same. It was confusing and scary.

But my mom stuck with him though this hard time. There was certainly an element of fear. She always watched me closely to make sure I was safe. Once, she and I climbed out the window in the night and waited in the barn for him to feel better before we came back to the house. I remember once even spending the night at a neighbor's house.

Another place I established beliefs and values was at South Buffalo, the one-room schoolhouse with a small entry. In the middle of the room was a wood stove. Next to the stove was a small table that the teacher would put the water jug on for water to drink. The blackboard was on the front wall with our individual desks all facing it. I was the only child in my class from first through fourth grade at South Buffalo, which made me feel very special. Such a sweet memory of being cherished.

I felt so special and important when it was my turn to raise the flag, lead the pledge of allegiance or pray for our lunches that we each packed and brought to school. In the eighth grade, I won the local spelling bee contest and was excited to go to the state capital in Pierre to compete.

We had a teacher for five years who was so determined to get to school to teach us, she came to South Buffalo from town and would shovel snow to get to school! In fact, she stayed in contact with me for years, sending Christmas cards until a few years ago when she passed away.

I had three good friends up until eighth grade. I know young girls don't do this much today, but I loved playing dolls. The four of us each sat in a corner of the small school room playing with our dolls and chatting during recesses.

At the little school we had an outhouse. In the winter we had to put our warm coat and boots on before we ran outside where the cold air froze our noses and eyes. Then we would run back to stand in front of the stove in the school building. Our teacher brought the water for washing in a jug and poured it in a basin for us because there was no running water in the country school. There was no bottled water then!

It was a fun and active time for me. We played outside during two recesses, and an hour at lunchtime. We would play "Annie, Annie Over," softball, and dodgeball. In the winter we would play "Fox and Goose" in the snow and bring our sleds.

It was a time of learning to deal with conflict. I remember feeling so bad after another student and I slapped each other's faces at competition time! We apologized later, but I learned not to strike out like that again.

When I was little, I could be naughty! And my mom could be harsh sometimes. When I wouldn't obey, my poor mom would chase me around the table with a paddle in her hand as I would run for my life. But mostly I was a good girl—at least I tried! I learned much about what being good meant from the little country church we went to three times a week. But more than that, the church is where I met Jesus.

The little Country Church sat on the northeast corner of the intersection with a few trees around the perimeter. Someone would ring the big bell before the services started. There were "his and hers" outhouses near the church. We would attend Sunday morning, Sunday evening and Wednesday night singing old hymns. We always ended the Sunday morning service by singing the hymn "Praise God from Whom All Blessings Flow." I often sat up front in the first or second pew with my friends. Sometimes we would start giggling—you know the kind—when you can't stop. The pastor would stop and reprimand us. Oh, did I get a paddling when I got home.

My mom was my first Sunday School teacher, and it was through her that I accepted Jesus at six years old. At home one night, after an evening service, I asked Jesus to forgive me and come into my heart. I could tell that Mom loved teaching young children, and I loved listening to her. She would prepare diligently at home during the week. Using flannel graphs and object lessons she made it very interesting for young minds.

I always looked forward each summer to attending Byron Bible Camp where we could swim in the James River, play games, and listen to the speakers. So much of the Bible became a part of me because we memorized so much Scripture. Memorizing was easy for me then; not so much now.

One evening the speaker encouraged us to dedicate our lives or accept Jesus as our Lord. I felt something inside and knew I was being led to rededicate my life to Christ. I had already accepted the Lord when I prayed with my mom years before, but I knew then that I needed to make this step in my relationship with Him.

Afterwards, a woman named Celia Gross met with me and shared the verse Philippians 1:6. That idea of God beginning a good work in me and continuing until it is completed connected with me and came to mean a lot in my life. Even now I think about how he began that good work in me a long time ago, but now he'll continue his work in me until it's finished and the Lord returns.

After camp and that experience, I felt more accepted by Jesus Christ than I did before. He seemed more personal to me. Shortly after that I was baptized in our church. It's a sweet memory, giving my testimony. Both of my folks were there. When it was over, I knew Jesus was with me, and I felt like a new person. He seemed closer to me somehow—not as distant.

Since then, I have been more sensitive in sharing Christ with others, and in high school God opened many doors for me to serve him through the youth group and with my friends.

On Being Remade

Along the early parts of my path, I acquired many true beliefs and helpful values. These were light, beautiful, and precious gems that Jesus put in my hand, and I promptly stashed into my pockets.

Sometimes I stooped down and picked up a rock by myself and put it in my pocket. It was usually heavy and cumbersome and didn't have value, but I kept it. These were untrue beliefs and unhelpful values that I would need to surrender to God so he could give back to me a precious stone instead.

Many of my beliefs, precious or worthless, came from that little circle of farm, school, and little country church. Working hard with my parents helped me to love work and the feeling of a job well done. Raising the flag every morning at country school and saying the pledge of allegiance instilled in me a deep love for my home and country. Praying before lunch each day with a different student leading allowed me to integrate my love of Jesus into my daily life in a seamless way.

In addition to working hard, loving God, and loving country, I also developed a drive to help people in their process of healing. My passion to care for people showed in that favorite book, with the little nurse character helping me realize that I wanted to make people well.

My imaginary restaurant was the beginning of my love for serving food to others. Mud pies aren't the most nutritious food, I suppose, but it shows how I wanted to serve others and meet their needs. Even as a tiny girl I loved to work and meet people's expectations—running a successful, if not tidy, business.

Through that book and my little restaurant, God was laying the foundation for me to meet the nutritional and health needs of others. I had no idea how God might allow me to bless people in real, tangible ways in the future.

Living through the hard times with my dad made me decide at a very young age that I would never drink. It made me very aware of when others are struggling with alcohol or have a loved one who struggles, and I empathize with what they are going through. Now I feel that I have an advantage in praying for people in those situations.

Through my early experiences on the farm, the little country school, and church, I acquired a deep belief that my value came from my performance. I have come to realize that this is a common thought. I had unreasonably high expectations for myself and others. Later in my life during farm crisis times and other difficulties, this led to habits of worry and concern—especially in finances and the safety of my loved ones.

Another area that God would grow in me was my security in him and a deeper understanding of his grace so that I could gain a new perspective on what my performance means and how I handle concerns.

I'm so thankful to see how God was with me as a young girl and had a plan to plant his truth in my heart and work on the untruths over time. His good plan was to help me understand his grace, peace, and sovereignty by meeting me in the difficult patches of road ahead.

Throughout my life, he met me in poverty, bankruptcy, MS, and depression, to teach me that he is all that I need.

2

Holding Jesus' Hand

After rededicating my life to Jesus, I began to sense that God was with me on the trail of my life. Life certainly became more interesting as I entered high school. I began to encounter more bumps and boulders that I navigated with the increased independence my parents allowed. True to my nature, I continued to stay busy.

I gained more responsibilities at home, worked jobs for other people, and had more freedom to spend time with friends at school and in the youth group. I also had more opportunities to serve others with my musical skills.

Through all these things, Jesus was preparing me for what was up ahead. It is so precious to see how even then, he was giving me what I would need to serve him in the future.

Young Blessings
• • • • • • • • • • • • • • •

Stifling giggles, my friends and I hid behind a tree in the summer evening as people walked, shopped, and mingled in the small downtown of Onida, South Dakota. It was harvest time and there were many strangers around. We waited for a break in the crowd and ran to another hiding spot so no one could see us barefoot and in our pajamas. I felt daring and adventurous running through the grass in yards and spying on people with my friends at night. We were giddy. That sleepover is one of my fondest memories of being a teen.

My good and giggling friends from the sleepover were one way God provided for me during this time. He also gave me good friends at school. We had so much fun singing trios together and having overnights. I loved feeling part of a group and being accepted.

God leading me to rededicate my life to Jesus just before high school was another blessing. I think about how he drew me to him in a closer way just as I was going to begin making my own life decisions. Because of that, I was able to practice relying on him for strength and direction during this crucial stage of life.

God also gave my parents the strength and resources they needed, even amid their own challenges. We were often together in the car driving to church where there were trusted people I could go to for advice and wisdom. Working the farm together helped me learn the values of hard work, diligence and completing a task. We had people in our church, school, and community to call on when we needed it.

Also, my skills were growing, with the help of other special people pouring into me. Goal setting, completing a task, work ethic, and excellency were developing during the busy days of high school.

High School Changes
· · · · · · · · · · · · · · · · · · · ·

A couple of big changes for me included having to leave my little, one-room school. The change from four students in my eighth grade to a "HUGE" school with 22 students in my class seemed overwhelming! I laugh now, but it was a real concern for me then thinking how different it would be. It wasn't long before I adjusted.

We also moved into a house in town that seemed so much bigger than the farmhouse. My dad continued to struggle with seasonal drinking, and my mom decided to move us all into town, living in a home next door to the sheriff for support. This turned out to be very helpful to our family.

Living in town also allowed me to be able to walk back and forth to school. The walk was six blocks down and one block over through the town's neighborhoods. I grew to know the houses well and waved at neighbors as I quickly walked to school and back twice a day. It was the kind of town where everyone knew everyone.

It was cheaper to eat at home, and I looked forward to having lunch with mom most days. I had to walk quickly to get there and back in time. Mom was always punctual with meals and lunch was at noon to give me time to get back to school. Mom was always happy to make lunch for me, which was always a surprise. It was special to come home to see her in the middle of the day. It was a connection time for her and me, talking about school and church.

Sometimes I would ask her to pray for a test because I knew she really did pray for me. At night I could see her from the hallway in her pajamas kneeling on the floor by her bed. It's a special memory for me, watching her talk to God in her room.

For as long as I could remember, my mom dreamed of becoming a nurse. When we moved to town, she took classes, got her nursing aide license, and began working at the local hospital. Oh, how she loved it! I knew she felt like she was contributing. Watching my mom model consistency and hard work impacted me, and seeing her achieve that inspired me. Her example instilled in me the importance of accomplishing goals.

Dad was giving me more responsibilities on the farm. In the summertime I spent time with him working in the field and learning from him. I felt that he knew that he could depend on me and that I would do a good job. Together, we plowed and windrowed hay and wheat. I also plowed and cultivated corn, although I didn't do very well with the cultivating.

When I was about five or six years old, I drove the pickup in the pasture, stretching my neck to see out the front window. In high school, I graduated to the tractor. It was a new IH 560 in international red with a white stripe. Dad was so proud of that tractor, and in his kind and patient way he taught me to drive it. It had a wide front and its deep treaded wheels seemed as tall as I was. Sitting up on it made me feel on top of the world! Together with that diesel engine we plowed 2000 acres together.

I still love to drive. Throughout my life, whenever I could drive, I took the chance. When Lee and I eventually got a riding lawn mower, I loved to mow the lawn. It was so much better than the old "pusher"! After we were married, Lee taught me how to run a much bigger tractor than my dad's, which allowed me to do the disking and harrowing. He also taught me how to run the combine to harvest corn. How thrilling to run those big machines. I wonder what my dad would think if he could see the big tractors today.

My parents didn't only teach me to work hard at school and in the fields. They showed me what it is like to work hard at sticking together even when life is hard. A sweet memory I will never forget is Mom and Dad memorizing the King James Version of 1 Corinthians 10:13 together.

There hath no temptation taken you but such as is common
to man: but God is faithful, who will not suffer you to be
tempted above that ye are able; but will with the temptation
also make a way to escape, that ye may be able to bear it.
1 CORINTHIANS 10:13 KJV

My dad repeated the verse and then would say, "I will never drink again." He continued to struggle, but I knew his heart was to follow God and to love Mom and me.

Life during high school was full of music; I sang, ran my fingers over piano keys, and blew through clarinet reeds. Senior year, my friend and I competed in the state competition on our clarinets. My band instructor helped our skills in teaching, communication, kindness, and musicianship.

I also had a wonderful piano teacher who demanded excellence. I had to memorize my pieces for recitals while my mother made me practice a half hour every day. I didn't like it at the time, but later I was glad that she insisted on consistent practice.

My youth group was a place I felt accepted. It's also where I began to grow spiritually in more grown-up ways. Saturday nights we would go bowling together or go roller skating. In the winter we went ice skating, where we held hands to make a long snake of laughing people and play *Crack the Whip*, trying to "lose" someone in the process! In the summertime we would sometimes do the youth group meeting outside and afterwards play games or have picnics.

In the summers, a college intern would help with the youth and learn from Pastor Bob Radke. Two or three summers during my junior and senior high school years, we had an intern named Don Hoover. Later in my life, I realized that both Don and Pastor Radke were tied to Lee and his family in interesting ways. Don married a girl Lee knew from high school, and Pastor Radke's wife led Lee to the Lord when he was nine years old at a home Bible study that Pastor Radke conducted. Lee's folks attended these studies and through them grew spiritually. Even before we met, Lee and I were spiritually influenced by the same people.

Another big part of participating in youth group was that we would travel to other churches and lead the whole service—singing, playing special numbers with me in a trio of girls, reading Scripture, and praying. I would also play the piano. Then the interning youth leader would give a message. It was fulfilling to see how God was using us teenagers in ministry.

Often, we had to get up very early on Sunday mornings to travel to churches as far as North Dakota. Once, I was babysitting on a Saturday night, and when I woke up on their couch Sunday morning, the parents had not come home. I didn't know how I was going to get to church, and the group was counting on me. As I wondered what I was going to do, my mom drove out to get me. Just then the parents came home. God did little things like that to show me that He was taking care of me and that I could trust Him.

On one of the trips to a church in North Dakota, I saw God's creation in the Badlands and felt a thrill at seeing the rugged beauty and roughness. It was mesmerizing with the gorgeous colors in the different layers of rock and soil. I was fascinated with the small lizards and birds and amazed at the big and powerful buffalo.

One year our trio sang at a contest in the county fair—we were a little nervous but enjoyed the day. The experience of singing at the fair and in many churches, and playing the piano, helped me feel more comfortable in front of people. It was stretching for me to be in front of people, but it prepared me for when I would need to speak in front of people as an adult. Even today I am much more comfortable in the background, but I have tools to communicate in front when it is necessary.

Jesus Leads the Way

Senior year was full of decisions. My boyfriend at the time was the nephew of the pastor's wife. However, the relationship was unhealthy. He was trying to manipulate me to do things I knew were wrong and said that if I broke up with him, he would kill himself. I felt like I was trapped even though he was placing on me a responsibility that wasn't mine.

One Sunday, my pastor's wife asked to meet me her after the service in Pastor Radke's office. As I walked down the hall, I had no idea what she wanted to talk about. She literally pleaded with me to break off the relationship with her nephew. That gave me the courage to break up with him regardless of the result. This was a major positive decision towards the direction I wanted to go in my life. I had stood up for myself and for what I believed. I was growing up.

Soon it was time to choose where I was headed for college. It was generally expected for women to decide from three choices: secretary, teacher, and nurse. I knew I didn't want to teach. So, with two options left, I talked with my parents and friends. Mom and I prayed, and I chose nursing because it enabled me to serve and to care. It felt like a natural choice since my sister was already a nurse and my mom had always wanted to be one. Following in their footsteps and in the dream that was born with my little *Nurse Nancy* book felt right.

Before I went to nursing school, I wanted to go to one year of Bible school. It was common for Christian young people to go to Bible school for the first year of college, and I felt that it was important to get a biblical foundation and worldview. My friend Virginia and I decided to go our first year to Grace Bible Institute. I already had a couple of friends who were going there. Within a week of graduating, at 17 years old, I was headed to Omaha, Nebraska with several friends. I had no idea that I would soon meet my future husband there.

A Pocket of Pebbles
. . . .

Growing up has many challenges for each of us, but I can see how God provided especially for me throughout my adolescence to prepare me for life. Because of his provision, I was able to make good decisions and practice the values and skills he would use in me for the future. Good friends, a family that loved me, opportunities to perform, times of service to others, and hard times in which I needed to trust him—these were all blessings I had in high school.

Somehow, despite all the blessings, my pockets were still weighed down by stones and pebbles of wrong perspectives.

As beautiful as growing up on the farm was, it had the downfall of training me to live to the very edges of life. I didn't know how to build in a "margin," which doctor and author Richard Swensen describes in his book of the same name. I lived that way for a long time: always working, never resting, always expecting exceptional work from myself and others.

Another weight I carried was an underpinning of performance that I learned from my church. Although they taught me to hide Scripture in my heart, pray, and serve, I didn't yet have a clear and deep understanding of grace, and I didn't feel confident in the security of my salvation. I used to wonder, "Am I good enough?" and "Is God pleased with me?" and I was determined to make sure the answers were "Yes!" But that put a burden of work on me that God didn't expect.

I also had a lack of confidence. Although I spent a considerable amount of time singing and playing in front of people, I was still shy. I don't know where this burden originated, but God would touch that area of my life too. He wanted me to be free to run and jump and play along the path, not trudge along hiding in fear.

These rocks weren't hidden from God as we traveled together, and he didn't want me to carry these burdens forever. He knew they slowed me down as I speed-walked home to eat with Mom. When I watched the Badlands fly by the window, God had a plan to prepare my heart for his truth. Even the fact that I didn't realize they were affecting me didn't stop my all-wise God from having a plan to free my pockets for more of his blessings.

Lee and I during our early years. We still love each other!

3

Ready, Set, GO!

Setting Out on My Own

. . . .

After high school graduation, God and I began to sprint down life's trail. I was young and full of energy. Two friends and I had applied for jobs as nurse's aides, and we left home that summer for Omaha, which was an eight-hour drive. I felt excited! Several girls went with me, all having the same plan.

We moved in with two other nurses at the White House Apartments and worked through the summer. I worked on the men's urology floor of the hospital.

One scary week, the news was filled with the killing of eight student nurses in Chicago by Richard Speck. The five of us were terrified and sure he was going to be in Omaha next. One night, we all slept in the same bed, mortified that we would be next. But as much as we were afraid, we also prayed together about it.

College Days and a Boy
• • • • • • • • • • • • • • • • • • •

School started in the fall. I was a freshman at Grace Bible Institute and that semester I took an Old Testament Survey class. We were seated alphabetically, which put Lee behind me in class, since I was a Walter and he a Williams. Apparently, he gave me a noticing glance that I overlooked completely. I found out later that he was too shy to ask me my name, so he went upstairs to the board where student pictures were posted with their names underneath.

He had this habit of tapping my chair with his foot, causing me to get distracted and turn around! He says now that he didn't even know he was doing it. But whether it was overt flirting or a simple nervous habit, it triggered a friendship.

The school didn't allow dating for the first nine weeks of school, so Lee waited until October or November to ask me out on a date. The first time he asked, I turned him down because I had to work that night. Lee thought that was an excuse, and still says that it was - with a grin. He got up the courage to ask me out again in December to go caroling with him. Our first date was on my birthday. Just before we all left for Christmas break many of us gathered around the piano singing Christmas Carols. He thought to himself, "She's a cool looking chick." After break, we began eating together at the cafeteria, and our friendship grew.

Meeting Lee along the road was exciting, but God and I had some talking to do before Lee would join me permanently on the path. In February there was a mission conference at college. Both Lee and I were questioning how our relationship fit into God's will for our lives.

Normally, we would wait for the other after the last class before lunch and eat together.

One day, during the missions conference, I went on down to eat without him. God was working on my heart. Lee came down later, saw me but didn't come over to join me. I didn't know it but God was working in his heart also.

I waited for him to finish at the head of the stairs and we both knew that God was at work. We went into the lounge area. No one else was around. In our discussion we both realized that God was working in our lives letting us know that he was to be first. We mutually agreed to break up because we wanted Christ first in our relationship. That was a difficult decision, but it was worth the effort to seek God first.

A few weeks later we did resume our relationship. Lee says, "That was a difficult time for me. I had not dated much at all before and had never broken up with anyone. But God used that time to cement in my life that he must be first in all instances." That was a lesson that he would learn in many other areas of his life. During that time, God assured Lee that I was the girl for him, although he didn't tell me that until later.

God had a full and fun year planned for me at Grace. I travelled with the college band, and Lee travelled with the chorus. I am so grateful for being able to attend Grace Bible Institute. Not only was I able to grow in my knowledge of God, but I also began to put my faith into practice in my young adult life.

The next summer before my sophomore year, my family had a reunion in Sioux Falls, South Dakota, and my uncle and aunt in Omaha invited Lee and I to go with them. The car broke down in Elk Point, Nebraska. We were sitting near a building that was under construction while waiting for the repairs when Lee told me that he loved me. It was the first time, and my heart skipped a beat.

In August 1967, I went home to South Dakota for a month before starting nurse's training. My dad was having drinking issues that summer, and I only saw him once during the visit. Lee had come for a time while I was there, and we both saw dad drive up in the alley in a brand new red El Camino. I hardly recognized him because of his drinking.

He roared off without saying a thing. We never saw him the rest of the weekend. I suspect he had come by to check out Lee.

Nursing School

Going to Immanuel School of Nursing, also in Omaha, changed my world. I dove into three years of intense work, starting with nurse's training followed by hours of study, walking to the hospital for long shifts of on-site training, and going to class.

One of my first experiences at nurse's training was when I was called in to talk to the administrator of the nursing school. She pinned me to the wall and shouted, "Why haven't you had your immunization shots?" I was mortified. Because of my mother's beliefs concerning immunizations, I had not had any shots. Mom had showed me pictures of children with very severe side effects after being immunized. To continue nursing school I had all the shots at once.

As my relationship with Lee continued to grow, I always looked forward to the weekends when he would come and get me and a couple of other girls and take us to church. We would often spend Sunday afternoons and evenings together.

It was during this time in the late 60s that there was racial tension across the country. Immanuel Hospital was in North Omaha, and the other nursing students and I would go up to the top of the roof and observe fires, gunshots, and graffiti on buildings. Tensions were so high that we would never leave the dorm alone and always cautiously traveled in groups. Looking back, Lee and I are very thankful to God that Lee never had an incident during the many trips he took through the most difficult areas of the city to see me.

Lee Joins the Journey
. . . .

A mutual respect grew early between us. Lee has always said how proud he is of me and impressed with my self-discipline during nursing school. Lee was continually amazed at how much time and energy I would devote to my schoolwork and big tests. For one major test I studied for 21 hours. I knew from growing up on the farm that to reach any goal I needed to be consistent, persistent, and disciplined. Lee helped me several evenings to study, and he was amazed.

I, likewise, was amazed by Lee's work ethic and commitment to getting things done right. I admired his ability to relate to people with ease and speak in public. We would need that love and mutual respect to get through the obstacles ahead of us.

Early in our relationship, God showed his grace to us very clearly. While we were still in school and before we got married, we found out we were going to have a baby.

We had to decide how to move forward in this. Should we hide the pregnancy? It seemed the logical plan, being unmarried and in Bible school. There were some couples that tried that, but we couldn't. It was a difficult decision to make, but we decided to tell our church and school the truth.

Our loving pastor and church in Omaha were forgiving. It was different when we stood in front of my home church in South Dakota and asked for forgiveness. Sadly, they would not allow us to be married in my home church.

But not everyone chose to treat us with judgement. Overall, the outpouring of love was immense. There was one dear man in the church who took us on a ride and expressed his love and care for us, even expressing displeasure at the church's decision. Most of the baby's needs were met through gifts. Lee even received a financial gift in his mailbox from a fellow student who had previously been judgmental toward him.

During this time, God gave me a special Scripture to comfort me. Psalm 32:1-5 says:

> *1 Blessed is the one*
> *whose transgressions are forgiven,*
> *whose sins are covered.*
> *2 Blessed is the one*
> *whose sin the Lord does not count against them*
> *and in whose spirit is no deceit.*
> *3 When I kept silent,*
> *my bones wasted away*
> *through my groaning all day long.*
> *4 For day and night*
> *your hand was heavy on me;*
> *my strength was sapped*
> *as in the heat of summer.*
> *5 Then I acknowledged my sin to you*
> *and did not cover up my iniquity.*
> *I said, "I will confess*
> *my transgressions to the Lord."*
> *And you forgave*
> *the guilt of my sin.*

We knew that it was likely that Grace Bible College would kick Lee out of college. It was a very conservative Bible school and that was the common response to our situation. Instead, the college erased a semester of credits from Lee's record, and he continued to attend for two more years to complete his degree. Through the experience, we received God's grace and mercy from so many of his people. Our response was simply to humble ourselves before our God and others.

After two years of nursing school, on the afternoon of September 13,1969, Lee took me to a beautiful spot on his father's farm to propose to me. We took a walk out into the timber about 400 yards from the farmhouse. Large, beautiful oak trees graced the area, and the birds sang. We often had taken such walks, both loving the quietness of the forest—walking, dreaming, and talking.

He had chosen a big old oak. We paused for a moment and then he bent on a knee and asked to marry me. Of course, I said yes, and he placed an engagement ring on my finger—a diamond that was an heirloom from his great aunt. It looked huge! We walked back to the old farmhouse, and I felt like I was walking on clouds. When we got back, his sisters had made a cake shaped like a ring. What a glorious day.

Lee and I married in June of 1970, and I graduated in August. I was so happy to have a partner to travel with who loved me, knew God, and would walk with me through life. The sun seemed to be shining down on the way before us.

Our first apartment was a third-floor penthouse in a building that was over 100 years old. There were so many steps! We made many fond memories in that unique home that had a circular living room. That was where we brought our first baby boy home.

God Provides Day by Day

Although the sun shone down on the path before us, our early marriage had plenty of hills to climb up and scramble back down. It was a time for us to learn to be a team, trusting God together. As we walked, a tree would be fallen in the path and God would provide a way around or under or through.

To say we struggled financially in our early marriage is an understatement. Lee laughs and says that he warned me that if I married him, "our chairs might be orange crates." He was almost right. The first seven months of marriage, Lee sold Kirby vacuum cleaners. In those seven months he made $700. As a result of that job and observing how other people keep their houses, he often says that he will never complain about my house cleaning! I am grateful for that.

On a hot June 13, 1970, I married my wonderful friend Lee that I love.

Another venture that we tried we call "the telephone card thing," which involved Lee traveling, spending quite a bit of money, and selling very little. Overall, the experience was stressful on the family because Lee was gone so much, and we had to float the travel expenses. We were glad when we were able to stop being involved in that. After that negative experience we said to each other, "We will never sign up for network marketing."

I remember that summer looking over the money we didn't have and turning to Lee while gesturing to a piece of paper. I asked him matter-of-factly, "Should we buy groceries this week or pay this bill?" It was the summer of 1970; I was just finishing training and he had two more years of college. We continued to live in the small apartment close to the campus of Grace University. Living one day at a time and trusting God for our needs was a daily exercise.

We were very young and terribly poor, but God was so faithful to us in the most tangible ways. We didn't always know where the gifts came from, but we always knew it was God blessing us. Several times we opened the mailbox and discovered cash. We might be running low on food, and someone would bring over groceries or money. Another time, someone came over and brought frozen meat for us. We were grateful for all of it because it showed us that God cared and was faithful to meet our needs.

When I graduated, I worked as a nurse, but did not get full RN wages until my State Board results were back. I was so fearful that I asked Lee to open the letter when it finally arrived. When he read that I had passed, I was so excited!

I continued working until Chad was born. Lee by this time was working at Northwestern Bell (NWB) Telephone and went full-time upon graduating. That corporate job put us in a much better financial position.

God was also using Lee to touch lives. During the noon hour at NWB, Lee led a Bible study where he saw some people come to the Lord, others grow, and some fall away.

It was a special blessing to see God work in that way.

Over a year later, we rented a house across the street from the Omaha Zoo. It was so fun to see the elephants and rhinos less than 100 yards away. Although it wasn't fun when Chad was napping and the peacocks got out of their enclosures and stood just across the zoo fence screeching until he woke up! That was 30 yards away! When he was a little older, Chad would tell people that we used to live in a zoo!

Learning to Be One

As we first started out, Lee and I learned about our similarities and differences, but not without being out of step with one another. The two of us have different personalities. I am the traditional Type A personality: very organized, self-disciplined, and driven to succeed. Lee, on the other hand, is more laid back and flexible. Like many married couples, our marriage includes one introvert (me) and one extrovert (Lee).

We both made adjustments. I was uncomfortable living life on a flexible schedule, not knowing when Lee would be home or what time dinner was going to be. Lee had to adjust to my need for certainty, plans, and schedules.

But there are also places where we overlap. We share many values including our deep love for people and relationships, and our love for our God. Although our styles are different in relating to others, we deeply love and want to see people grow. Even now we have patients, roommates, church friends and family relationships that stretch back to college days and our first years of marriage.

It was worth the investment to learn to work with our different strengths and weaknesses because God had a plan to build us into a better team.

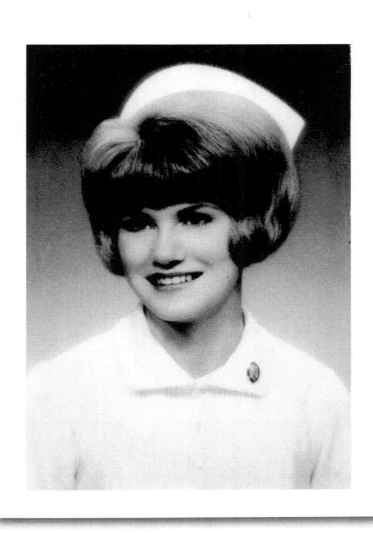

A milestone achieved when I graduated as a nurse in 1970.

Loss and Change
• • • • • • • • • • • • • • • •

In 1971, having Lee in my life was a gracious gift to me as the path ahead held loss and change. Like a fog rolling over the road ahead, we lost my dad tragically to complications of rheumatoid arthritis.

Two years later, when I was nearly due to have our second child, the house we were renting sold, and we had to move. Again, we saw God provide. We discovered that it was cheaper to purchase a home than to rent, and we bought a brand new house in LaVista, Nebraska. We moved within a week of Heather being born. It was a blessing, but also a stress on us to have to move.

Our new house was right next to a stream, and across the stream was a park. Not a bad setting for two farm kids! But living in town felt a little strange to me. There was always so much going on, and I had another kitchen window just 10 feet from mine! I love people, but I also cherish quietness and space.

In 1975, the fog thickened when my mother suddenly passed away of a massive heart attack. I was shocked and felt lost as a 25-year-old with three little ones and both my parents gone.

In the fog, the road got bumpy as I struggled with motherhood. There were parts of being a mother that didn't come easily to me. I had to learn patience the hard way. Being raised basically a single child (my two sisters were 12 and 20 years older than me) it was difficult to adjust to the sibling quarrels of my children. Lee helped me to understand that this was normal, was not a reflection of my mothering, but it was still difficult. He grew up with three siblings all within five years of each other.

During this time of my life my self-expectations were near perfection. My house had to be perfect, clean, and picked up. It was the same with my children. I was devastated when anyone just dropped in.

My young mother's Bible study was helpful. There were about five of us. We studied I Timothy word by word, which was enriching and stimulating. Our group grew very close. We all had children nearly the same age and all faced similar issues. We desired to be good mothers and good wives. Those were precious times.

Back to the Farm

When our children were one, three and five years old, we felt God calling us to take a turn in the path and leave the city to go back to the family farm to raise our children. Lee had a good job and NWB wanted him to move up in the company, but he was unhappy with having to spend so much time away from me and the kids. Working in management and on salary meant long hours. He was also associate pastor of a small church and busy nearly every evening.

One weekend Lee took the kids for a walk in the park. The neighborhood kids came out and were talking. They were nice kids, but their underlying attitude and perspective clashed with what we wanted our kids to know. He came home and said "Our kids will probably spend more time with them than with me. I want to be able to teach them the values we grew up with." At that point, we started praying about moving back to Lee's family farm.

We didn't take the decision lightly. We wanted to follow the path God had for us and wanted to know that He was leading in that direction. Lee and I thought about and prayed about the decision for over a year before we moved. By the time God opened the door for us to rent land near where his dad and brother were farming, we were convinced this was what God was asking us to do. There was no question in our minds that God led us back to the farm. We didn't know it then, but we would need that confirmation to carry us through the very difficult years to come.

The first house we moved into was a small, old farm-house. It wasn't very tightly insulated and before long, the rats moved into the basement! Then we found rat droppings across our bed and even upstairs. That was the last straw. We quickly moved out and stayed with Lee's folks until we exterminated them and Lee cleaned everything.

It was 1976 when we moved to that small house with Chad, Heather, and Brent. We called it "The Grant House" near the small town of Grant, Iowa. It wasn't too bad finan-cially at first and Lee, his dad, brother, and I enjoyed work-ing together to run the farms. Lee's brother Stephen loved the milk cows, so he oversaw that. Lee's dad and Lee did all the row crop farming: soybeans, corn, and hay. They both had stock cows, and Lee had lots of hogs. They got along great as a team.

Something fun Lee's dad did for the 200th birthday of our country was to enter several bicentennial parades. He put together a four-wheeler kit and connected three little red wagons to it. Each of the grandkids sat in a wagon while Lee and I dressed up like pioneers and walked with them. Lee's dad was so proud!

The first year on the farm we decided to attend a church we had never been to before. It was a good respite for us since we had been so active in the church in Omaha while we were both working. We needed a break.

But the respite didn't last long before we started having a Bible study in our home. We are so thankful that we did. Some of those attendees have been our friends for over 40 years. I developed mentoring relationships with two young girls, and I still treasure those relationships today. After a year, we began having services in our home as we saw many people come to know the Lord and grow spiritually. Even-tually we moved that house church into the Legion building in Grant.

After our third year of farming, the farmer that we rented land from gave the farm to his newly married daughter and son-in-law, and we moved to another farm. We moved to "The Knight Place," in Iowa, about 15 miles from the Grant farm, in the spring of 1979.

Personal Struggles

• • • • • • • • • • • • • • • • •

Although we enjoyed it, those first three years of being back to farm life left me exhausted and drained. My movement through the days was frantic just trying to keep up! Life was so busy for me with the kids and trying to keep up the garden, cleaning the house, and working part-time. I would get home at midnight and still need to wash clothes and the cloth diapers. I was trying to be a support to Lee, and I knew he was trying to support me, but I was just so tired. That was life.

Many times, when I felt like I couldn't keep going, my father and mother's work ethics carried me through. I worked so hard, even pushing the lawn mower while carrying baby Brent on my hip. But we didn't have a work-life balance. It was all just life. And it was busy.

I tried to keep a consistent quiet time, but it was difficult. I was vulnerable to feelings of not measuring up—especially to the expectations of Lee's mother. Perhaps they were self-imposed expectations. She always had a large garden and was an early riser. On the other hand, I was working part-time as a nurse on the 3-11p.m. shifts, and taking care of the three babies. My garden wasn't spectacular.

Lee couldn't help me with my work. He spent long hours farming. Sometimes he didn't come home until 7 or 8 at night. As things got tighter it was often 10 or 11 at night or later. Admittedly, my situation is common for young moms, but I felt the real pressure to measure up and a keen perception of my lack of performance.

Those pebbles in my pocket were having a greater effect on my life, and I was getting exhausted carrying the burden of performance around with me. I could see that I was not handling the pressure well. I could be testy and impatient. I know now that part of the picture was that I was dealing with severe PMS each month, but back then I just knew that there were times when I couldn't hold it together.

For Lee, the work of the farms was immense. Lee's father was not as established as my dad had been. My dad was in his late forties when I was born. In addition, we had a dairy which requires morning and evening milking, hogs and crop work. At "The Knight Place" we also had more miles to travel to the farm.

The difficulty was that the two farms Lee was working (160 and 240 acres) were 15 to 20 miles from his dad's 439- and 240-acre farms. There were no cell phones then, and Lee couldn't tell me how long he would be out.

I don't think I understood the extreme pressure Lee felt at the time. He could see that the finances were not good. His brother saw it too and left the farm in the early 80s, moving to Colorado. His dad started working at a factory and driving a truck. Lee just pushed himself even harder to make the farm work. I found out later that he didn't tell me about the times he was in danger. There were nights when he worked the tractor between 9 p.m. and 12 a.m. and would fall asleep. He would wake up and not know where in the field he was. He was so exhausted. God was gracious and he never had an accident.

Lee and I prayed a lot about the friction we felt, but we also fought. If Lee didn't get home in time to take over for me with the kids before I needed to leave for work, I would lose it. Then there were the times that I didn't know where he was or when he would be coming home. I knew the dangers of farming, and I was concerned about accidents with the equipment. I'd pace and watch out the window. Oh, I can't count the times I planned his funeral!

Life was becoming too much for both of us. But it wasn't too much for God, if only we would hold his hand on the bumpy trail.

It was a challenge with our schedules, but we did try to have family devotion time each evening.

Spending time with the Lord helped, and although we were overwhelmed, our faith and commitment to each other was strong.

We also had supportive people around us. During that time, God provided strong relationships with two other farm families that have lasted for over 40 years. Our kids were similar ages, and we had a lot in common. Whenever we could, we would celebrate our birthdays together working around farming schedules. We still do to this day!

This time in my life began and ended with a sprint along the path God was walking with me. I started out in a car full of girls and progressed to living on a farm with my life partner and three beautiful kids.

God had been faithful to me the whole way. From the sunny and exciting patch of the road when I started college and met Lee, through the fog of losing my parents, and onto the bumpy changes motherhood and farming brought, he always provided. Now I was sprinting again, trying to make it all work with my expectations of myself and what I thought others expected of me, and I could feel the pressure building. But God had a plan to teach me another level of trust in him.

Me with Lee's 1972 tractor. I have always loved to drive.

Lee taught me to drive the combine during our year of farming together.

4

Tackling Hills

Two are better than one,
because they have a good return for their labor:
If either of them falls down,
one can help the other up.
But pity anyone who falls
and has no one to help them up.
Also, if two lie down together, they will keep warm.
But how can one keep warm alone?
ECCLESIASTES 4:9-11

The hill was steep as Lee and I climbed: slipping on pebbles, bumping into one another, grabbing an arm to steady the other and ourselves. Every day we pushed hard along the path, working to love the kids and each other, striving to provide and to keep the dream of the farm alive.

The fog of grief was lifting as the loss of my parents stung less, and God's light dappled the trail here and there. I knew of his faithfulness, but I was still learning to walk in it.

Life at Home
• • • • • • • • • • • •

Life on the farm with the family seemed to change every day. The kids were always growing and needing different things. The farm work was intense. After staying home with the kids for the first five years, I went back to nursing.

The days were long. Lee was gone all day working and farming, and Lee's mom watched the kids if I had to leave for work before he got home. The day didn't end until I came home at midnight.

But we all started the long day together at breakfast. Sometimes I'd cook oatmeal, other times pancakes and eggs. The kids would get dressed before they came out and greeted me in the kitchen. Then we would all eat.

As much as he could, Lee tried to hold their hands and pray with them before they rode off on the bus for the long days. The bus left at 6:45 a.m. and they didn't get home until 5 p.m.

There were some good conversations with the kids at breakfast. When we lived at "The Knight Place," and Lee and I were working the farm together that year, Lee told the kids that he and I would sort the hogs while they were at school. Brent who was about six years old said, "Daddy I don't think you should do that." Lee asked Brent, "Why?" Brent said, "Because you yell at mommy."

What we learn from our kids! That was a wakeup call for Lee. After that, he was much more careful with his words and tone. He realized that if he didn't learn to rein it in, the kids might not want to work with their dad.

After school and on weekends, there was always farm work for the kids to do. Moving to the farm helped them learn to be good workers with good work ethics. They helped with the livestock and went out and gathered eggs. They had chores to do and responsibilities. I always wrote a list of things to do, and as they got older they had more chores outside.

In the spring, our family picked up branches together and pulled them away in a red wagon.

We moved cattle for Lee and his dad. When they were smaller, the kids opened gates. As they got older, they helped Dad and Grandpa on horseback.

Lee taught Chad how to drive the tractor and do field work. The first time Chad drove a tractor on the road a couple of years later, I was sure he was going to roll into the ditch! I was scared. He seemed so little. He didn't crash, and I learned that it's so much harder to watch your son drive a tractor than to do it yourself!

But even with all the work, we found fun and made time to be together even though I used to say "Rest doesn't come before the work is done. And the work is never done!"

The kids looked forward to Lee coming home because we had fun when we were altogether. When I saw Lee coming home, I would sing, "Daddy's home!" and the kids would rush outside and run right into his arms, hugging his waist or legs.

When we lived at "The Grant House" and "The Knight Place," we liked to go to the lake on hot summer Sunday afternoons. We blew up old tire inner tubes and it was always a special time as a family.

We also liked to go to softball games. Lee was on a league, which was a hot item in the summer. Every small town had a team and we made time for Lee to play and for us to come as a family to watch. The kids would watch and play with the other kids.

Sports became big in our family. This was new for me. I wasn't athletic, but Lee was. His whole family was athletic. In high school, he played all the sports available. He even went to state twice in track. Lee's mom played basketball, and his dad played basketball and baseball.

I never heard of girls playing basketball. When Heather got to high school, I thought to myself, "She'll be a good cheerleader." But she played basketball and became a star on her team, making the varsity team as a freshman. She lettered in both basketball and volleyball and ran track every spring. The boys played football, basketball and track.

When Lee was in school, his dad was never able to come to his games because of the dairy, so we tried to go to as many of our kids' games as we could. The trouble was, I fell right to sleep during the ballgames. I'd be watching the action on one side of the court and doze off. When I woke up, I'd be looking the wrong way! I was so embarrassed. There was another family with a similar struggle. The husband couldn't stay awake either. When we see them today, we still laugh about it!

Sports was a great way to interact with our kids. Once during basketball season of his senior year, Brent came to Lee with a problem. A new kid came in and took over his spot. It was usual for parents to gripe in the bleachers about the issues their kids had with the team or the coach, but Lee decided not to do that. Instead, he told Brent to talk to his coach and ask what he needed to do to get his place back. We tried to allow learning experiences for the kids, to prepare them for their future.

One difficult lesson for Chad was in waiting. His freshman year he wanted so badly to play football, but he had just grown six inches in eight months the previous year. Lee told him that it was too risky for him to play after growing so much so fast. Lee got him into weights to give him the strength to handle the sport the next year.

Golden Year
• • • • • • • • • • •

From 1979 to 1981 we lived at the house and farm that we called "The Knight Place" because we rented it from a family with that name. That house was the backdrop for one of the most enjoyable years of our marriage, when I took time off of nursing and helped Lee farm.

When we look back, that was our favorite year farming. We loved working together. Sometimes we split the tasks while other times we had our own.

I prepared the soil for planting while Lee planted in the spring. He taught me how to run the combine in the fall to harvest and he hauled grain in. Sometimes we switched and I hauled the grain in while he combined.

Farming is a full and active life. I must have carried a small pond full of water in five gallon buckets. I got our kids and the neighbor kids involved by helping me walk beans, cutting the weeds out of the soybean fields.

I took a class at the local co-op called Baby Pig Husbandry on how to take care of baby pigs and their mommas. I learned how to clip teeth, clip tails, give shots, and castrate the little boys. I took over the farrowing house, where they were born and lived with their mothers for a few weeks. To this day Lee says that I did a better job in the farrowing house then he did! I loved it!

Once, after I prepared the baby pigs to be taken from their mamas, it was time for Lee to take over. One sow had her babies in a muddy lot, since the farrowing house was full. Lee pulled the babies out of the mud and placed the small pigs safely in a bucket. While he was heading to the shed, the mother headed for him! He put the bucket between him and the mother, but she didn't stop. Lee slipped and fell on his back in the mud and soon the mother was on top of him with his forearm in her mouth. He was in a muddy and dangerous mess! She didn't clamp down, fortunately, and for some unknown reason. I think it was the Lord who caused her to suddenly turn and go back to where her babies had been. I shudder to think how that story could have ended differently.

A Determined Hope

Pressure Mounts
• • • • • • • • • • • • • • •

As much as we loved being back to farm life, there were challenges. In 1981 we got hailed out twice. In 1982 we had no rain and our farms produced only 60, another 30 and another 5 bushels of corn per acre. It should have been 150 bushels per acre. Our schedules were full to bursting, but as hard as we worked, the money wasn't coming in. My nursing kept finances reasonably stable, but things were tight. We had been in difficult financial spots before, but it was still a strain.

With our physical, emotional, and financial resources stretched to their limits, sometimes our tempers flared, and our emotions were so strong that we really wished we hadn't said what we did. That is when we would agree to take a half hour to do something else and discuss it when our minds were clear, and our emotions settled down.

This is an example of one of the principles that we enacted early on in our marriage. The saying "Don't let the sun go down on your anger" is from Ephesians 4:26. We tried to talk things out right away, and after we did, it would usually come to the place where we would be honest and humble enough to say, "I'm sorry. Will you forgive me?" That last part was very important: asking for and receiving forgiveness.

Early on, we tried to keep the stress from the children, but they picked up on things. At one point, Lee felt that since the kids were going to face the same situations when they were grown, it would be better for them to see by example how we dealt with difficult things. That perspective helped us to discuss life in front of the kids. We did not want to argue in front of them but wanted to show them how we were making decisions handling struggles.

When we needed to talk privately, we went outside. Other times we waited until the kids went to bed. Our main way of

58

talking was to go for a walk.

There were times that I would lose it and be impatient. I had horrible migraine headaches that would paralyze me, yet somehow, I was able to push through and continue working. For two to three weeks out of the month I struggled emotionally, spiritually, and physically and didn't understand why I felt that way. Much of my life I struggled with feelings of inadequacy and self-value. Later I learned that much of it related to severe premenstrual syndrome.

5

Valley of the Dark Ages

When we reached the summit of the hill we were climbing with God, Lee and I looked down into a dark valley. It looked scary, but there was no alternate path because God had led us here. There was nothing to do but move forward with the faith we had, not knowing what was ahead. We call 1980-1990 "The Dark Ages" because it was so difficult, but God never left us and had lessons for us to learn.

It was 1980, and Lee was working full-time at a factory during the days. Then he worked three farms at night. I was working part-time as a nurse, all while the kids were still very young. Lee would be gone for long hours—whole days and nights really, and I wouldn't hear anything from him. I stayed home worrying. I was always certain there was an accident with the tractor, or that he was stuck somewhere in the timber. Long before cell phones, it seemed like there was nothing for me to do but wait and worry and pray. I prayed a lot!

And it seemed I worried for good reason. Lee stretched himself so thin that he sometimes didn't remember going through a field with the tractor. When he got this tired his strategy was to stop the tractor, keep it running and take a 15–20-minute nap in the field only to wake up and continue.

Financially, things were getting tighter and tighter. The crops were failing, and the stress was mounting. I started working nights and expecting Lee to come home to take care of the kids on those evenings. Those were the worst. With the stress and the fright, I would be so happy and relieved to see him one minute and then get so angry with him the next.

At one point, I had a plan to take the kids to Kansas City, Missouri, find a full-time job and a babysitter so I could make more money. Lee and I went to a counselor instead, and we decided to stay together and keep working at our life together. Lee quit the factory job for the family's sake, even though it didn't seem to make financial sense. Once, Lee went outside to the front of the house and stood outside on the sidewalk. He was brutally honest with God yelling, "I am sick and tired of what is going on!" There were no lightning bolts of judgment and at that moment he knew that God accepted him regardless of what was going on outside and inside of him. Then Lee was able to go back into the house and love me even though the tensions were all still there.

July 4, 1980 came with a bang, but not because of any glorious fireworks display. A violent wind tore through our area, destroying some of the windows in our house and flattening a good crop of corn that stood five feet tall—about half their mature height. Most of those corn stalks eventually straightened back up with a crook in them, but when Lee harvested that year, he picked through a field of curved stalks and salvaged a disappointing crop.

We faced a worse tragedy the next year. Lee planted corn

in the early spring, and by May it was eight to 10 inches tall and looking good. But on June 1, a violent hailstorm tore the bark off trees and mowed that crop right down to the ground, washing it away.

Like many farmers, Lee is an eternal optimist who figures that with more work and a little more time, everything will work out fine. So, after letting the field dry out from the hailstorm, he bought more seed and replanted the corn and soybeans.

"This crop won't be what it could've been," Lee said the night he finished planting, "but at least we will have something."

But later that night, tragedy struck again. Another violent hailstorm blew through. This time there were no cornstalks to attack, so the hail went after the soil, washing away all the newly planted seeds.

Lee and I went out to assess the damage. We stood together in the barren field, holding hands as we looked at our beautiful crops reduced to bare ground. We quietly cried together as we saw how quickly all our work and money had turned to nothing. As we wept, we asked, "God what are you doing here?"

Two years later, a wet spring made for a late planting season. When the crop was finally in the ground, it refused to rain, and we had drought. At the time, we expected 150 bushels per acre for a corn yield. Our north farm produced 60 bushels, middle farm 30 and our south farm, the largest at that time, produced 5 bushels to the acre. To make things worse, it was all moldy.

In 1982 Lee worked a full-time job at a factory, farmed 600 acres of his own rented land and helped his dad with 600 acres. He would leave at 5 in the morning and get back at 11 or 12 at night. It seemed like I hardly ever saw him. I don't know how many times I planned his funeral—we didn't have cell phones then! I knew he was tired and worn out, but I don't think I knew the extent of the stress and pressure he was feeling.

It's times like these that can test the strength of a partnership. Tragedy could have caused us to turn on each other. We didn't want that. God had allowed our relationship to grow so that, as Solomon's words in Ecclesiastes describes, "Two are better than one." We had to help each other up and keep each other warm during the Dark Ages of our life. I'm so thankful neither of us had to weather that time alone.

The next year, in 1984, we filed for bankruptcy. We didn't know what else to do. It had gotten to the point where some days we had to decide whether to pay a bill or buy food for the kids. I never bought any new clothes for myself, and I would patch Lee's and my jeans and my kids' clothes. I always got used clothes for the kids to wear for church and school.

Even after the bankruptcy, Lee kept working the farm for a couple of more years. Then, in 1986, Lee's dad died of cancer. That broke us. We lost the farm and had the farm sale the next spring.

We were done, depleted, and the question loomed, "How do we build back up again?" Thankfully my nursing job enabled us to survive.

Head in Hands

· · · · · · · · · · · · ·

Lee looked at bankruptcy and losing the farm as a personal failure. His heart ached at losing his father's farm and he felt like the world was judging him for being a poor farmer. He would sit in the back of church with his head in his hands feeling ashamed.

When tax time came, Lee couldn't face going so I went on my own. I'm not a numbers person at all, but I went anyway. It was so depressing. The interest rate at the time was 21%. We just couldn't make it. For several years in a row, we had to borrow money to pay the taxes or our kids would starve.

On one point, Lee and I went to the government office to see if we could get food stamps. When they asked about our situation, Lee was honest and mentioned that he had savings bonds in the kids' names. He had purchased them when working at NWB years before. They said we had to cash them in first before we could get any assistance. He said, "But they're not mine." It didn't matter, and we walked out praying, "God, you have to provide another way."

Losing the Farm
• • • • • • • • • • • • • •

I remember having to say goodbye to the family farm—the land, the pond, the timber, and the fields. We worked and endured so much to keep it going when the farm crisis hit during those years of hail, bad crops and even worse economy. Many families left before us, but Lee and I kept on.

Far from being a relief, bankruptcy felt wrong. It was against our nature to give up on the farm and on the people who had invested in us.

It was a heart-wrenching time. More than just the loss of money and the effort it represented, it was the loss of our livelihood, home, and memories. But not of our honor. Early on, we determined to pay the debts back someday, even though we were not legally obligated to, and we weren't sure exactly how that was going to happen.

Lee and I owed several businesses—the biggest being the farm co-op which was $8,000 at the time of the bankruptcy—a daunting debt to us. It took many years of work, persistence, saving and building a successful Juice Plus+ (JP+) business to save enough to pay it back, but it was worth it.

Years later, Lee walked into the co-op with a check for the full amount and handed it to Randy Daugherty, the new man managing the business. Randy looked at him from behind his desk, looked down at the check and looked at him again and said, "Lee, you are an honorable man."

Later, Randy Daugherty called Delmar South, the man

who ran the co-op back when Lee and I declared bankruptcy. The next time Delmar saw Lee he said, "Lee, that's what Christians do."

These experiences could have tempted us to hold onto every penny, afraid bad times would hit again. But God has worked a miracle of perspective in our minds and hearts that allows us to hold what we have with open hands.

Because of that perspective, I believe that if something happened with our finances and things changed, I could go back to being very frugal again. I don't think I could say that if we had given in to the temptation to see money as a source of happiness.

We chose to hold on to Philippians 4:12-13:

I know what it is to be in need, and I know what it is to have plenty. I have learned the secret of being content in any and every situation, whether well fed or hungry, whether living in plenty or in want. I can do all this through him who gives me strength.

Glimmers in the Valley

God always provided hope through our struggles. He gave us relationships to minister to us, food to nourish us, and money to pay bills.

Our pastor, Dan Butler, impacted us greatly. His friendship, love for the Lord, and love for our children was heartwarming. He was a good listener in my struggles and a good friend to Lee.

One of the biggest contentions between Lee and me was that there was no time for dates. God provided Pastor Dan, who was willing to watch our kids when we really needed time out together.

Much like the one I had in the city, God gave me another Bible study with some other young women who were very impactful and encouraging to me. I love the relationships we built around church and Bible study. Some of those relationships remain today.

During this season of daily practice in trusting God to provide, we received gifts of food and money, which were enough to pay a bill or buy groceries. We were so thankful whenever God provided this way.

Finding Fun

• • • • • • • • • • • •

During all this difficulty and crisis, we made some wonderful family memories. When we lived at "The Dewey Place," the kids wanted us to have a special anniversary. After school, they prepared a picnic for us along what we now know is Williams Creek. They led us past the farm buildings and down to the creek where they had a little fire started and a picnic all laid out for us. It was a glorious time eating hot dogs and marshmallows.

The few vacations we took needed to be after planting and before harvest. One of our favorite vacations was to California to visit my sister and niece in 1982. We took my nephew with us, camping along the way with the kids in tents and Lee and me in the car. Chad was 12, Heather 10, and Brent 8.

On that trip I had my first time at sea. My sister was dating an engineer who built an ocean-worthy boat. It was a thrill when we went out five miles and couldn't see land!

I liked to watch on the beach and get tan while Lee and the kids played in the water. The kids loved body surfing. Lee loved it too until a wave tossed him around. He somersaulted, faceplanted on the ocean floor, and came up with a scraped face!

There was a parade in beautiful Monterey, CA. Our daughter Heather loved animals and was not afraid of snakes. Someone in the parade had a great big snake in a basket and she went up and held it over her head. When I saw her, I just walked the other way. I can't handle snakes!

We went to Fisherman's Wharf and watched the fisherman coming in. They gave us a couple of fish and we took them home and filleted them. That was a treat. We saw fireworks over the bay during an Asian celebration. On the way home, we stopped at the four corners of Arizona, Utah, Colorado, and New Mexico and stopped to visit friends. Such sweet memories.

Redemption Along the Road

At the time, we didn't know how God would redeem the difficulties we endured in the valley, but now we can look back and see how he redeemed our struggles.

We saw his eternal power in the ministry he allowed us to do even during that difficult time. During all the busyness of farming and raising the kids, we were still able to be active in our church: Sunday school, vacation Bible school, and Bible studies. One year we had a study in our home with several couples. One very young couple attended. The husband, Bill, was a new believer, and his wife could not figure out what had happened to him. She thought he went off the deep end religiously. We invited them to come. Lee told me later, "Sherry fell in love with you," and within a few months, she came to Christ. To this day they are very close friends of ours.

The farm crises drew Lee and I together when it could have driven us apart. Although those difficult years affected our marriage, we never considered divorce. Divorce was not an option. Going through that experience would help us later with my MS diagnosis.

I saw more examples of how I could depend on God and his faithfulness because he met us again during the farm crisis. I learned to trust him with my physical needs of food and shelter because he was faithful in providing. And because of going through this hard thing, I can encourage others in difficult circumstances to trust God with their daily needs.

God met us each step of the way, giving us wisdom when the kids needed it, ideas on how to navigate our frictions, provisions when things got tight, and grace when the world wouldn't give it.

Did we trip and fall during our journey through the Valley of the Dark Ages? Yes, but God was allowing us to learn to pick each other up and look to him for our provision. We were ready for what was over the hill in front of us because God had grown our faith.

6

Retracing Steps

"For I know the plans I have for you," declares the Lord,
"plans to prosper you and not to harm you, plans to give you
hope and a future."
JEREMIAH 29:11

In February of 1987, the bank took back Lee's family farm and sold the equipment. It was devastating. Not only did we lose our income, but we also lost a part of our family's history.

That metaphorical path we were on ended abruptly with thick timber ahead and no path. Light dappled here and there through the branches. We stared into the dense forest looking for a sign of a trail, but the tangle of underbrush was thick and undisturbed. It certainly didn't look on the outside like we were on our way to a prosperous future.

But God. We knew he had a plan. We just didn't know what it was yet. Still, we had to do something. We couldn't just stand there in the forest in the valley. We had bills to pay and kids to care for. But where could we go from here? It seemed the only way forward was backwards, and we started to backtrack together, trusting God would show us the way.

I thought that the door for us ever farming again had closed, but there wasn't much time to grieve our losses. Financially, we were at square one after declaring bankruptcy, so we had to keep moving. Money was tight and we went into existence mode, working day by day to pay bill by bill. There wasn't time for big visions and dreams.

It was one of those times in life where the old saying was true: we couldn't see the forest for the trees. Life was taking care of today's needs, walking the next steps God showed us. It was much like the hunting caps with lights that Lee and the boys used. They only lit up the next 10 steps ahead. I think of the words in Proverbs 16:9:

> In their hearts humans plan their course,
> but the Lord establishes their steps.

We were living in the house we call "The Dewey Place" on rented land. I went back to nursing, driving 20 miles each way, and Lee got a job in a jacket factory 30 miles away. The kids continued school, sports, and activities.

There were people in our lives who were supportive and others who were not. One man would listen while Lee talked out his thoughts and feelings. He gave Lee a job helping at his veterinarian clinic, which gave the family insurance. He became one of Lee's best friends.

Others responded with more judgment about the loss of the farm and the bankruptcy. It was difficult to know that there were people looking at our situation and judging our character for it.

We both felt very alone and fought depression. We didn't want to talk to people and were tempted to withdraw. But there were others struggling too, especially neighbors, who felt comfortable coming to Lee with their burdens.

One man who lost his farm came after dark, while Lee

was harvesting, and unloaded on him. Surprisingly, this was part of God's healing plan. In comforting others and seeing them reach out, it helped Lee to reach out in his own struggles. And it helped to see our struggle was being used to help others. Once you go through something difficult, you can help people around you in their struggles.

For me, reading God's word and praying by myself was my relief. God would fill up my soul and restore me in those times. Psalm 119:105 describes how God's word affected me:

Your word is a lamp for my feet,
a light on my path.

Daily Trust

Lee's father had only been gone for about a year at this time, but his influence on Lee is timeless. I admire Lee's positive attitude. He was raised with a dad who was always positive. Up to the point of his death, Lee's father was always looking ahead and asking, "How can we improve?" I think his influence on Lee was a rock to stand on.

We had an advantage because we had gone to college and made a living away from the farm for a few years. We had a better idea of what we did and didn't want to do in our work. Many others didn't know what to do besides farm work.

The factory gave Lee great promises, but no follow through. They gave him more and more responsibility, but not the authority to accomplish the goals. His manager was constantly changing his role and it was frustrating for Lee.

Meanwhile, I was enjoying my work in home health care, although the commute and the hours were intense and the days were long.

We started looking to buy a home on an acreage that was closer to work. After one possibility fell through, a friend mentioned that a neighbor might be thinking of down-sizing. After getting to know the man for several months we made an offer on his six-acre land. The man received another offer, but he decided to sell to us for our terms because we "would make this a home, not a summer home."

We took possession in November. There had been no updates to the home for 50 years, which meant repairing where a water tank had been upstairs, metal cabinets in the kitchen, and an old pantry. We began remodeling and moved in the next February.

Lee had to leave the jacket factory job in January 1989. While he was on unemployment, he worked on the house. Since the house was small for us, that summer we put on a 16-by-30-foot addition.

Soon he found work as a carpenter with three believing men who taught him much about the craft. During this time, I was asked to be a manager in home health care. I stayed in that role for 13 years.

Chad graduated from high school in May. The house still needed work and the whole family helped. While the boys helped rip out walls, Heather and I took off wallpaper. So much wallpaper! We even textured the ceiling after the leak was fixed. Even the neighbors pitched in to help. I remember painting the day before graduation for the celebration. Lee was up on the roof painting the upper story, and friends came over and put in the kitchen sink.

The work was worth it. We lived at "The Acreage" for 26 years, making many memories. We built a barn that burned down. Then we built another one. Lee was always up to something. Once, he bought a one-room schoolhouse that was going to be torn down for 200 dollars.

Our neighbor asked him, "What are you going to do with it?" He said, "Move it up to my place." The neighbor just shook his head saying to himself as much as to Lee, "If anyone can do it, you can."

When they brought it up with a John Deere tractor, the

school house got stuck between the house and the garage. It sat there for three weeks before we could move it. Eventually, it became a cottage with a bathroom and a kitchenette, where Lee's mom lived for three years.

"The Dewey Place" where we used to live was in a valley so you couldn't see the sun rise or set. I loved that on "The Acreage" you could see both the sunrise and sunset. I had to get used to the traffic, but being only 12-15 miles from Atlantic, Iowa lifted much stress off both Lee and me.

In the fall, Chad went away to Grace University which was only a little over an hour away. It was still such a big change for our first child going to college. I remember the five of us parking in the back and helping take everything in—including an old, fleecy brown chair we bought him from Goodwill. He must have used that chair for 10 years! When it was time to leave, we all hugged him and got teary. Soon it was time for Heather and Brent to do the same. Heather to Northwestern in St. Paul, Minnesota and Brent to Northwestern in Orange City, Iowa.

While the kids were in college, we kept in close contact through letters and calls when we could. All three kids had jobs and worked especially hard. With each of them working and the small amount we could help with, none of them had to take out a loan.

Chad played basketball for two years in college. Lee loved to see him play but didn't get to go very much.

Heather was in Minneapolis/St. Paul, five and a half hours away. It was difficult to leave her, and we cried when we dropped her off. That first fall, I was determined to attend parents' weekend in October. As we got closer to the day, a snow and ice storm started coming in. I didn't care and I said, "We are gonna go." The next morning, I stood by the door with my suitcase looking at half an inch of ice and eight inches of snow. That day there were power outages and trees falling through roofs. We didn't make it to Parents' Day.

Brent went to play football at Northwestern. It was a beautiful campus with Christian influence. We were officially empty nesters.

They all came home for Christmas each year. One year, a tall guy brought Heather home for Christmas. He was interested in her, but I think she was oblivious. We didn't see them for Easters, but we did in summertime. The boys worked for Lee, especially Brent. The three of them worked at Raccoon River Bible Camp where Lee, our kids and grandkids used to go when in high school.

Growing Inside and Out
· ·

Looking back, I am so thankful for how God was faithful to us during that time. He never left us abandoned and used the trials to draw us closer as a family and to trust him more. Bankruptcy could have driven Lee and me apart. Instead, God's grace was to grow us closer together.

While God helped me to trust him with my life and eternal destiny as a child and young adult, he taught me other things during and after the farm crisis. I learned how to depend on him for practical needs, be more patient, and have grace for myself and others. He also taught me how to better trust Lee.

I love Philippians 4:19, which says:

> *And my God will meet all your needs according to the riches of his glory in Christ Jesus.*

Over and over, he provided food and money when we needed it. Sometimes it was enough to pay a bill; sometimes it was for groceries. With each gift and provision, my trust in his faithfulness grew.

I have learned patience the hard way. Being raised basically as a single child, it was difficult to adjust to the sibling quarrels and conflicts of my children. Lee helped me understand that that is normal and that it was not a reflection of my lack of mothering.

During this time of my life my self-expectations were near perfection. My house had to be perfect, clean, and picked up. Same with my children. I was devastated when anyone just dropped in. God has grown in me an ability now to let some of that go. Now I love it when others drop by unexpectedly.

My expectations of others have changed too. I used to get so frustrated when others didn't meet my expectations. I have learned and continue to learn to be more forgiving and accepting. Lee has encouraged me that I have really grown in this area.

I've also learned to trust Lee more. Watching Lee in the difficult times and seeing his unwavering understanding in God's sovereignty and provision has helped my trust in him to grow.

All of this prepared us for the blessings and trials that were ahead, as well as the people God would bring into my life to bless. I knew in a deeper way that I could depend on God because I had seen him provide in the large and very smallest of my needs.

After we turned back from the path's end, which was losing the farm, we came to the other end of the valley and started on a slow, financial incline. God's faithfulness and the hard work he provided for us to do was followed by the sun starting to shine. The stress started to lift a bit, but there was still no time or energy to consider the future beyond the everyday. That's okay. There are times like that in life, and that opportunity would come.

We are so proud of our three kids (L-R) Brent, Chad, and Heather.

Part Two, God Refines

7

Bridge Over a Barren Hole

The LORD is my strength and my shield; my heart trusts in him, and he helps me. My heart leaps for joy, and with my song I praise him.
PSALM 28:7

A Barren Hole
. . . .

Since growing up in South Dakota, I've seen many lands with different beauties. Colorado has striking mountains. Montana has wide lands and sprawling skies. But of all the places I've been, Iowa has my favorite beauty. I love to watch the green rolling hills and trees transition through the seasons to the winter harshness. The hills become steeper then slope down to shallow spots. You never know what's up ahead or around the corner, but you always know that it will be consistently Iowa.

God chose for me a beautiful road that is much like an Iowa trail. Full of beauty and challenges, slipping through season after season, different in circumstances but always the same in the company of my Savior and Lee, the partner God gave me.

As our kids were moving into adulthood and we turned a corner on the trail, an unexpected obstacle spread out in front of us. The timber fell away, the trail stopped, and we stared into a large barren hole. It seemed strangely out of place in the lush Iowa timber. There didn't seem to be any way around it and beyond was a stormy land we couldn't decipher.

It was 1994, and we were happily exhausted from our daughter's wedding and welcoming a new family member in our son-in-law. Life was full of new beginnings. So, when I woke up three days later and felt a tingling sensation in my legs, I thought I was simply tired from the activity of the wedding. I tried to rest, but the feeling didn't go away. Within a week I was extremely fatigued and was having difficulty walking. I knew that something was very wrong.

Our family doctor scheduled an appointment with a neurologist in Omaha. Sitting across from him, Lee and I heard the life-changing news: multiple sclerosis. He explained that my spine had multiple lesions causing the loss of feeling in my legs. We tried to take in the information that the treatments available at the time were all experimental with serious side effects.

From my years as a nurse, I knew the disease all too well and tried to push away the faces of patients who had descended into the pit before us. I imagined myself in a wheelchair and then the thought, "I'll never be able to hold my grandbabies," brought stinging tears and sadness.

We drove home in silence, our faces wet, our minds full as we stared down into the metaphorical barren hole in our path and looked beyond into the stormy future. What would this mean for us? How would we cope? How would

Lee manage to care for me as my condition got worse?

Over weeks and months, we wrestled with the news and tried to understand what all this meant for us and our family. I became convinced that soon I would be on my way to a nursing home, riding in a wheelchair.

My grandkids make me smile when they play and fish at the cabin pond.

Bridge to the Other Side

I'm so thankful that I didn't experience months of sorrow and wallowing in fear, loss, sadness, dread, and uncertainty. Yes, I did feel all those things, but we began to pray and seek God for answers to this new challenge. After all, we had seen God's faithfulness in more than 20 years of faith challenges along our path together: losing my parents, surgeries, lost crops, and financial stress.

I knew the answer was Jesus—the one I gave my life to at camp when I was only 13 years old.

Then the nurse in me began researching my new diagnosis. My sister Jan, who was also a trained nurse, had a gift for researching as well, and began in earnest to find resources and information about MS that might help. She found a nutritional book with a diet specifically for MS, which I began to follow.

Our mother had been a good example to us in researching our health, as she had also chosen to look for natural ways to support her body when we were younger. So, when God began to lead me to treat my illness naturally as well, it was familiar to me.

Within a matter of weeks, I felt a peace from God on the direction that I should take for my health. As Lee and I prayed, it became clear in my heart that God was asking me to continue to do the things I was already doing to support my body naturally and not take the treatment available at the time. We decided that the many side effects were not worth the possible benefit I might receive.[1]

I had become the patient. After years of treating others, I realized God was now caring for me and working a determination in my heart to do the things I needed to do to stay healthy despite the diagnosis.

Nutrition and movement were the bridge God provided to help Lee and me cross the barren hole of the diagnosis and navigate the storm of this illness brewing on the other side.

Between the diet, which included juicing, a shoebox full of supplements, and a determination to do all I could to keep my body active and to maintain all the strength that I could, I began putting into practice what I felt God was asking of me. Remembering my mom's journey with supplements and nutrition, and her determination, bolstered my own.

At first, I decided to continue to work as a nurse and juice

---

1 *Choosing to treat my multiple sclerosis naturally and without medication was a very personal decision for me based on my personal health, perspective and the treatments available at the time. We worked closely with my healthcare providers to understand the options I had. I am not suggesting that anyone should make their own treatment decisions based on my experience. Each person has to make their own personal medical choices with their healthcare provider based on their own situation and the treatment options open to them.*

once a week. I noticed that on the juicing days I felt much better. Eventually, I was juicing several times a week—faithfully buying, washing, cutting, and putting my greens in the juicer to watch a small amount of juice spill out. Then I'd take the juicer apart and clean up the green splatters on the counter and in the sink.

It was a messy business. More importantly, juicing was taking the little time and energy I still had after working and dealing with the MS symptoms.

And now, looking at a sink full of dishes, I wondered how I was going to keep that promise to myself. Even though my mom had done the same, eating raw and steamed fruits and vegetables, some days it just seemed impossible to get all the produce I needed into my body. To compensate, my shoebox was stuffed with supplements that I took faithfully. Even with all that, I still needed help.

Simple Splatter Solution

That's when I was introduced to Juice Plus+ by a friend of a friend. I was not interested. The thought of taking "just one more pill," made my eyes water, as I was already faithfully taking my supplements and juicing.

Then Lee said, "We need to try this. It makes sense to me." I wondered what made JP+ any different from what I was doing now. Why was this capsule better than any number of supplements or whole food products on the shelf or in my shoebox? Even though I had hit my limit and really didn't want to try something new, I started taking JP+.

Those friends eventually introduced me to Wendy Campbell, an RN. I related to that, and she told me that JP+ was a way to flood my body with fruits and vegetables and that there were scientific studies that backed up its value.

I had more questions than I was willing to hear answers. Then one day while I was working at the hospital, I saw a medical journal on the doctor's desk with a JP+ research article.

I knew that this journal was a trusted source for medical professionals. Not only that, but it was research about the problem my body was facing—immune dysfunction. I was so impressed that the product had actual medical testing that showed how effective it could be at putting the body's immune system in balance after 80 days, measuring the bioavailable nutrients in blood.

I knew that my immune system needed to get back in balance since MS is a result of an imbalanced immune system. I thought of all the supplements I was taking and knew that not one of them was tested at this level.

My guard began to relax as the simple, natural solution of real food bringing health to bodies in an easy-to-take form began to make sense to me! This was no supplement like I had ever taken. This was real food that was simple to take and was researched in a way I could respect.

Plus, it didn't require all those dishes! Eventually I would discover how much mess, time and cost I would save with this solution and how effective it would be for my body. I began to see how the products fit exactly with what I felt God was leading me to do and how they would be easy to integrate into my everyday life.

After being on JP+ for only a few weeks, Lee went to Kansas City Kansas for a three-day conference. When he came home, he noticed me "zipping around" the house, reminding him of the energy and drive I had before the MS diagnosis. We both were amazed at the improvement in how I felt.

Tiny Victories
• • • • • • • • • • • • •

It wasn't long before our son Chad and his wife Karen were due to have our first grandbaby. Josiah was born in June, and we went to the hospital in Lincoln, Nebraska to meet him for the first time. As I walked in, I could hardly wait to sit down and hold this precious little boy after thinking I would be too ill for this moment. Such a sweet time.

I have many happy memories with all fourteen of my grandchildren who surprise me with their wit, charm, and personality. Together we've thrown snowballs and made snow angels. We've baked, gone on trips, and completed family projects. Some of them have worked for us in summers, and Lee and I have sat in bleachers for athletic events during the school year. I've often watched them play from our back porch.

When my granddaughters were little, we had what they call "tea with Grandma." I kept a collection of "Abraham Lincoln" dresses, big hats, and clip-on earrings for them to dress up in. They would clamber up the wood farmhouse stairs and put on dresses that were far too big for them while I set out fancy tea and treats in 19th-century style.

When the grandkids got to be nine years old, we started taking them on our business and speaking trips. I got this idea from another dear couple that we had grown very close to. Most of the time, we had two or three kids go together on a trip. The last grandchild brought a friend along. It was fun to watch the cousins bond on these trips.

We tried to make the trips fun and educational, and no two trips were ever the same.

Our trips took us to many places. We went to Spook Cave at a campground in northern Iowa, to Wisconsin to see a Victorian house, to see locks and dams, and the Effigy Mounds.

One time I drove slowly through Anita State Park, Iowa, and they stood up through the sunroof. We counted the deer and rabbits we saw along the drive. Sometimes we would take their bikes to the park and ride the back paths.

Those experiences allowed us to get to know our grandchildren as individuals. We thoroughly enjoyed the bonding we experienced as grandparents with every one of them during these trips.

I didn't get to spend much time with my grandpa, so it's very precious to me that Lee and I are able to be an active grandpa and grandma. MS has not stolen that joy from me, and I am so grateful for how God has taken care of me.

Continuing the Journey

Taking JP+, as well as staying active, allowed Lee and me to climb out of the hole of learning about the MS, continue through the storm of figuring out how to approach the illness, and continue our life path together.

I remember when I decided to support my health by taking JP+ and changing the way I ate, Lee said that I wouldn't have to do it alone. He was willing to eat what I ate so I didn't have to make separate meals. That has brought us closer together, and his support encourages me to keep going.

My special word for 2019 was "hope." Sometimes it takes work to hold onto hope. In 2015, 21 years after I was diagnosed with MS, the neurologist said that I had "progressive MS." Right then I decided to block the word "progressive" out of my mind and continue the path I felt God had given me. Then, two years later, the doctor told me there were no active lesions, which meant that the disease was not progressing!

That's not to say that I don't have hard days. Though not progressive, the MS has caused permanent damage to my spine. Some days I have pain. Especially when the weather shifts, and we get what my daughter-in-law calls "a bear-cat-weather day" when it seems like the pain blows in with the wind.

I would much rather be serving, comforting, and caring for someone else's needs, but often these days God has me doing a lot of self-care. Exercising, eating well, resting. It can be discouraging for someone like me who doesn't want to sit down until all the work is done! That's when I need a good serving of hope. On those days, I like to nibble on a verse like Psalm 28:7:

> *The LORD is my strength and my shield; my heart trusts in him, and he helps me. My heart leaps for joy, and with my song I praise him.*

When I struggle emotionally, I often have a heart-to-heart conversation with Jesus. I also reach out to others. I don't want to just think about myself and this body. I feel better when I serve. The struggles I've gone through have built in me an empathy I could not have had otherwise. My goal is to do something each day to build loving relationships with the people God puts in my path.

8

Sun Shines on a
New Path

However, as it is written:
"What no eye has seen,
what no ear has heard,
and what no human mind has conceived"—
the things God has prepared for those who love him—
1 CORINTHIANS 2:9

Walking back together seemed like a useless exercise. Hadn't we seen these sites before? That little tree, that big rock, the little mole's hole; it all looked familiar. We were back to our tight schedules, even tighter budgets, and the smallest of energy reserves.

We worked to stay in the moment and find joy in the days, but it felt like we weren't making any progress. Little did we know that God was building in us the strength and experiences that would allow us to follow him on an adventure we would never have imagined for ourselves.

And then the road surprised us. We saw a light beyond the trees, and when we pushed the branches aside, a new path spread out in front of us. A path of opportunity which included Juice Plus+.

New opportunity amid illness

When JP+ entered our lives, I was working full-time, and Lee was working in carpentry. Financial stability seemed a long way off, but we were working at it together. I wasn't sure how long I would be able to work, now that we knew I had MS. I had seen the end of the road for that disease in patients and was still wrestling with my potential future.

Despite the numbness and tingling from waist down, fatigue, and bladder issues, I still poured myself into my work in home health care. The migraines I struggled with since I was in high school still bothered me, but I kept going. In fact, I was surprised to find out that not everyone with migraines can keep working through the pain. Once, I went to a continuing education class for nurses. Many struggled with migraines, and they were going around the circle asking how people coped. Some said they had to go home from work, others had to lie down or take medicine. I was surprised because I usually just got sick in the bathroom and continued to work. I guess I didn't think I had any other choice.

I determined to do all I could to keep my body active and to maintain all the strength that I could to reduce the inflammation and continue living an active life. I did lots of walking: sometimes down the road or around the section of the neighborhood we lived in, many times with a neighbor friend. One fun activity was to pick up pop cans in the ditches on the roads with my grandson Josiah. Walking in the fresh air lifted me up emotionally and physically.

Soon after I began taking JP+, I started to feel the changes inside me. The longer I took it, the more I could feel the differences. Before JP+, I was always so tired and would just kind of drop after work. Now, I had more energy and was able to move better.

Lee saw the difference in a couple of weeks. I didn't notice until about a month of taking it. It made such a difference. Lee and I have this back and forth where I say that without JP+ I would be in a nursing home. Lee gets prickled and mutters under his breath, "No you wouldn't. I would take care of you."

Soon after starting JP+ Lee and I decided that I should be a Partner, after a call with my up-line's sponsor, Wendy Campbell. It allowed us to get the product for a better price, but Lee saw more than that. He said, "I think this is something you could do!" I wasn't so sure, but I tentatively agreed.

I was surprised Lee thought JP+ business was a good idea. Another experience with network marketing had been negative, and we said to each other, "We will never sign up for network marketing."

Years ago, we participated in what we now refer to as "The telephone card thing," which involved Lee traveling, spending quite a bit of money, and selling very little. Overall, the experience was stressful on the family because Lee was gone so much, and we had to float the travel expenses. We were glad when we were able to stop being involved in that venture.

How glad I am that Lee put our declaration aside and listened to what JP+ had to offer and encouraged me to give it a try! He heard something different in the JP+ presentation and our experience has turned out completely different. I love what the company stands for and respect how it is run.

I had no idea what a blessing the business of JP+ would be to me and to others.

I never thought I would be able to play with my grandkids in the snow.

Finding my Stride
• • • • • • • • • • • • • • •

Lee was right. It was something I could do, and I could do it with passion. I was so excited about what was happening to my health that I was already sharing with my friends and family. I wanted others to know how flooding their body with fruits and vegetables could help them too.

People started responding. My daughter-in-law began taking it before our second grandchild was born. In fact, all our kids started taking the product, and I've always felt good about my kids and grandkids receiving the benefits of fruits and vegetables.

We worked the business together; we always have. Lee brought many people to me from work. He would meet people that didn't feel well and would share a bit about JP+ and ask if I could give them a call to explain more. Lee is such a natural people-person who feels comfortable sharing our story. I am more of a detail person who can give insight to the specifics, send resources, and follow up. We make a great team in that way.

Since my schedule was so full, I determined to do something every day. At first, that was all I could do. I did a few presentations, but not many. Lee would do some also. God seemed to place Lee and me together with people who needed help. Soon, I had some prospects who became Partners, and that was the beginning of my JP+ business growing.

Although we enjoyed the JP+ work, it was a learning experience for both of us, and it was still work. It was challenging for me to call people, but I decided to pick up that "600 pound" phone and a smile.

I didn't used to be a goal-setter, but I became one. I wrote down goals every month. I decided to make three phone calls each day. And I made sure to simply follow through. That's how my business started to grow; excitement, God appointments, and completing small goals.

Once Lee and I made a big list called my Memory Jogger. I still have it. We wrote down 100 names of everyone we knew. My goal and my excitement to tell people about what had happened to my health through JP+ helped me to overcome the barrier I had to picking up the phone. I wanted to talk to people.

I remember saying over and over to the people I cared about, "I'm so excited about something I just learned about. Can I send you some information through the mail?" We didn't have computers at the time, so we had to mail the information packets, tapes or videos. I also would invite them to meet a JP+ friend on a three-way call and I would talk with them about their health with someone in my team to teach them about how JP+ could help them too.

A Short Rest and Then Growth

· ·

About a year after I became a Partner, my MS symptoms and working full-time were overwhelming, and I decided to pull back on growing my business. It was like taking a short rest on a bench near the path. I told my sponsor that I would continue to support my current customers, but that I wasn't going to try to grow my business anymore. That lasted about three months.

Then God set up a couple of situations where a customer came to me wanting to become a distributor. This created a momentum that was contagious, and I felt a desire again to see the business grow.

Lee and I saw the value of sharing JP+, and our passion to see people become healthier was only growing. Sharing the goodness of fruits and vegetables with enough people one person at a time was slow going. More and more people wanted to hear my experience, but public speaking was not anything I was excited to do.

It was a major challenge for me to learn to get up in front of people. When they were small, I told my kids that I would never speak in front of a group; so, when I agreed to put together my story and share it in front of people, I surprised myself and them.

I knew I needed help to put it together, so I recruited my sister Jan to help me with the message and Lee to make the PowerPoint slides. One of my team members asked me to share in a small setting in Kansas City. It was small enough that I was willing try, and it went surprisingly well.

I began sharing my story more and more. In fact, I have shared all over the U.S., and was more than a little nervous when I got up in front of over 100 people! I was glad to share with other people who were impacted by MS how JP+ improved my life and health.

I'll probably never be a great orator, but I've grown into

public speaking. Most people don't know that I must write down everything I'm going to say. I learn it very well before I present so it doesn't appear that I am reading or have portions of it memorized. I had to find what worked for me.

When I realized that many people struggle with immune system issues, I felt so thankful that God was using my struggle to help others, and it became something I could not resist talking about. It was just like Romans 8:28:

And we know that in all things God works for the good of those who love him, who have been called according to his purpose.

Added Blessings of JP+

Beyond the benefits to my health and our finances, JP+ gave Lee and me many more blessings we didn't expect.

I have three nieces who I didn't have the opportunity to get to know earlier in life. We lived thousands of miles apart, but because of JP+, I was able to develop close relationships with them. They became some of my early Partners. It felt good to connect with family again. There have been many years we got to see them twice at conferences and sometimes more in our travels.

We have also developed a huge number of family-like relationships with other JP+ Partners.

I have learned so much about business principles and relationship principles. We have travelled all over the country and have friends we care about wherever we go. Building the business has had a huge impact on our lives in how we function, serve, live, and enjoy life.

Oh, how we have enjoyed life!

I think back to when I was diagnosed with MS and the fear that I would never be able to hold my grandchildren. Just several years after we started on the JP+ journey, we had several grandchildren over at "The Acreage," and I played softball outside with several of them. They hit the ball while Lee and I pitched and fielded the ball. I really tried to chase down those balls. Another time I was out in the snow with several of the grandkids and we flopped down and made snow angels! It felt so good to actively play with my grandkids, and those memories bring such joy to my life now.

Unexpected Successes

After three years of sharing JP+, I stepped down to part-time nursing. About that time, the Juice Plus+ company assigned me a mentor or business partner. Jerry Waites helped me so much. When he passed away a few years ago, I was devastated.

With Jerry's guidance I became a National Marketing Director (NMD) after five years. It was such a wonderful moment for me to be in front of the annual conference and share my story. That was a turning point for us. Three years later, Lee also became an NMD. How fun it was for him to cheer me on and then for me to cheer for him.

Things were looking up financially for us and career-wise for me. I was able to capitalize on the benefit package of the company, which was remarkable–major medical, dental, health, and bonuses. Plus, my income from JP+ surpassed my nursing salary.

I had finally found my place encouraging healthy living; whereas in nursing, I felt more and more like I was participating in sick care. Now I really felt like I was helping people be proactive with their health.

By the time I became an NMD, Lee and I decided I should retire from nursing and focus on JP+. I had already moved from part-time to working as an occasional night nurse so it didn't seem like it would be a difficult adjustment, but it was. Very difficult. At the next bend in the road, I would learn about my identity, where it was, and where it could be.

Determined Steps

. . . .

It's strange to think that the sunbathed path we happened upon was made possible by bankruptcy and a health crisis. That's probably because it wasn't by accident. God led us there after preparing us in the climbs, valleys, retraced steps and stumbles that came before. Proverbs 16:9 describes it well:

In their hearts humans plan their course,
but the Lord establishes their steps.

Letting go of our dream of the farm had allowed us to embrace the blessing of JP+. And there were more steps to come. More steps of learning, growing, and unexpected blessing.

9

Sitting in a
Solitary Spot

He lifted me out of the slimy pit,
out of the mud and mire;
he set my feet on a rock
and gave me a firm place to stand.
PSALM 40:2

We had been moving quickly along a smooth path without many rocks or obstacles. We could see far and
wide across fields and rolling hills. Our legs were getting
stronger and our hearts growing stamina.

Lee and I were enjoying working together again in our
JP+ endeavor. It had been a long time since that favorite
year working the farm together and it felt good to work
side-by-side again.

The sunny path that included Juice Plus+ and all the
opportunities it provided allowed our lives to become full of
activity. We saw health in my body, joy in caring for others,

and provision for us financially.

It made sense to retire from nursing when my JP+ business income surpassed my nursing income. The Juice Plus+ Company provided excellent medical benefits now, and I enjoyed encouraging people to be proactive with their health rather than waiting to bring it into their story once they were ill.

Most people we had met who retired from their former careers to focus on JP+ were elated after they made the change. We assumed my experience would be the same when I retired from nursing. We thought leaving nursing would allow me to run even faster along the sunny path. But my experience was a bit different than we expected.

The path that looked like a straight shot through the rolling hills and meadows dipped and led me on a small trail to a depression surrounded by trees. As I arrived at the solitary spot, I felt an extreme exhaustion and sat down in the stillness.

A Deeper Identity

Sometimes life stops before it moves on. This is what was happening to me. Retiring did not initially feel to me like a blessing. Rather, it took me to a place of deep questioning of my life purpose and my identity. Change often triggers questions and feelings, but this was different than any of the other changes we had gone through.

Physically, I was tired and feeling the effects of MS on my body. I had significant fatigue and changes going on in my body. Plus, I began to forget things that I usually had no trouble keeping track of. It was getting more and more challenging to push through the discomfort.

Sleep was challenging. I would fall asleep and wake up at midnight. Then I couldn't fall asleep again. Questions began to crowd my mind. Was retiring really the right thing to do? What would we do without the steady income of my job which got us through so many difficult years? What if the JP+ business didn't work out and we couldn't make ends meet? Would we be able to contribute to our kids and grandkids if we didn't have a steady source of income?

And then another, much deeper, line of questioning crept in. Who would need me now that I didn't have patients to care for? Who was I if I wasn't a nurse?

Not a nurse. That was the core of my struggle. I was having a crisis of identity and, as a result, my mind and heart were full of emotions I had never experienced before. I thought of the many hurting people I wouldn't be there to care for anymore. No one would need me to chart their progress, get their meds, or draw their curtains. I was afraid of the future and grieving the past.

I felt lost, and I wasn't sure what to do. I had been a nurse so long that it felt strange to wake up and not have a name tag to wear or patients to greet. I had always been driven and busy, and now I could barely get through the days. I couldn't see a reason to get dressed.

Nursing had filled a deep need in my life and had been a major part of my identity. It filled my need to care. How could I survive with this void?

As a string of sleepless nights dragged on into weeks of sleeplessness, I began to feel the deep fatigue that comes with insomnia and this vague feeling I now know as depression, loss, and anxiety.

I liked the mornings better when the sleeplessness drove me from bed early. At least then I could read, pray, and journal. Then the time that I used to leave for work could slip by quietly unnoticed. And those mornings were the beginning of my healing from depression—when answers began to fill the void.

The answers came in those times alone in the quiet when no one needed me. They didn't come in one dramatic moment like when you pull back a curtain in a dark room and it floods with light. It was more like the dawning of a day. As I continued to pray, read, keep a journal, seek God for what he had in this difficult time, and even thank him for the hardships, something wonderful began to happen. God began to teach me.

In my retirement, I had time to spend reading and reflecting that I never had before. It was in the stillness that God was able to show me important truths that would free me from bondage as well as be better able to help others. It is like the Psalmist quotes:

> He says, "Be still, and know that I am God;
> I will be exalted among the nations,
> I will be exalted in the earth."
> PSALM 46:10

Several important resources came my way. One came when Lee's Aunt Janet realized that I was struggling and gave me a list of "Who I am in Christ" statements written by Neil Anderson. She told me, "Say these out loud every day." I did. It is amazing that something as simple as meditating on the truth of who I am could help to change my identity and beliefs about myself.

I realized many things in my times alone. That God was sufficient. That I did not have to make everything happen. That I couldn't measure up on my own, and that it wasn't my job to be in control or figure out the finances. As I learned to walk in these realizations and let God do all of that in my life, I began to be free in new ways.

Another breath of fresh air came sitting in the recliner out at our acreage reading Kay Arthur's book *Living Behind the Mask* as well as her *Names of God*. These helped me realize who I was and who God was and made a big difference in my perspective. That's when I realized something very important. I am not my work.

The Lord led Lee and me to read Neil Anderson's book *The Bondage Breaker*. It helped us to focus on who I was in

Christ. It took about 6-8 months, but I finally broke free from the depression.

Lost and Found
• • • • • • • • • • • • • • •

Yes, by leaving full-time nursing, I had lost something precious that had filled a void that God created in me—the desire to care for others. I also felt a sense of loss deeper than that. A loss of myself somehow. Somewhere along the way, I had begun to think that my work was who I was—my identity. Who was I if not a nurse? And that was exactly the question I needed to be asking.

The answer lay beneath the mask of performance I lived behind so much of my life. It took the loss of my profession for me to take off that mask. Then I began to see who I was, who God is, and that led to insight into my true purpose. Instead of the "worry, worry, worry" I had lived in without understanding God's sovereignty and sufficiency, I began to live in a new freedom knowing he is in control, and he is enough!

I can accept where I'm at today and rest knowing that the result is not up to me. Sure, there's a fine line between trusting God for the result and walking the steps with God to get there. Life is still full of activity, but when my perspective shifted, I began to see the difference between fruitful activity and the fretful kind.

An attitude of gratefulness started to grow within me. I was choosing to be grateful for the difficult things in my life. In my journal I wrote, "I choose to thank you for my weaknesses, my infirmities, my inadequacies (physical, mental, emotional) ...for the ways I fall short of what people [hold] as ideal...for my feelings of helplessness and infirmity, and even my pain and distresses. What a comfort it is to know that you understand the feeling of my weaknesses! ...and that in your infinite wisdom you have allowed these in my life so that they may contribute to your high purposes for me."

And on another day, "Thank you that many a time my weaknesses cut through my pride and help me walk humbly with you...then as you promised, you give me more grace—you help and bless and strengthen me. Thank you for all the ways I'm inadequate, for they prod me to trust in you and not in myself...and I'm grateful that my adequacy comes from you, the all-sufficient God who is enough!"

Nothing about my circumstances had changed. I could see my nursing days waning. What the MS diagnosis meant for my life continued to be an unknown. My physical and even emotional struggles were very real. The memories of lean times were still very vivid in my mind. But inwardly, I was being remade.

Now I knew that I was more than a nurse. I was Jeanie, God's special creation. And leaving nursing couldn't change that.

The depression began to lift, the anxiety to dim, and I was again able to pour into my JP+ business. The business began to fill the God-given need I had to care. I began to think of the business as a "ministry" and the healthy effect I saw in people's lives began to drive me to continue reaching out to more and more people with the product.

My favorite part of JP+ is the opportunity to provide customer care and encourage my Partners to grow their businesses and to continue in personal growth. I have all this hope to share!

I wrote in my journal, "It is so rewarding to see people's health so positively affected—this is what keeps me going Lord. It is your business—I am so driven to do it and yet Lord please help me to keep things in right perspective."

As hard as it was to begin to thank God for the hard things in my life, I can't imagine our story now without those hard things. Everything I've endured has allowed me to go beyond sympathizing with people who struggle with their health to empathizing with them.

Whether it's insomnia, depression, anxiety, pain, loss, or

life change, I know how hard it can be and that there is still hope. I love to share hope. That's the difference between sympathy and empathy. Sympathy allows you to acknowledge what others are experiencing. But when you empathize, you can share what has grown inside of you because of the pain. For me, the pain has grown hope.

Emotional struggles are normal. We're all on a life-long journey to grow in the health of our body, soul, and spirit. For me it was the time to press in and look for answers. It was worth the effort.

Embracing the questions and feelings that change brought and facing them was so important for me. If I had stuffed them and not searched for the truth, I might have missed what was going to fill the void. For me, the uncertainty was rooted in how my need to care might be filled. I was also grieving the past and finding the courage to embrace the future.

After experiencing depression, I am better able to serve the needs of the people who come along my path and empathize with where they are at emotionally in a way I couldn't have before. I was able to bring encouragement and hope to them in a more wholistic way.

I know that after I walked through my difficult journey with depression and loss, I had more to offer to the people I served through my business than I did before. I had developed a whole life perspective on health that went beyond nutrition. I truly wanted to see people begin to be healthy from the inside out.

Pouring Out my Pockets

In my little story about the path God has me on, I turned my pockets inside-out and let the pebbles of performance and false identity drop to the ground. I didn't need them anymore because now I knew that the results of my work did not have to be perfect for him to accept me. I also knew that I was more than a nurse and that God accepted me for being Jeanie, his creation.

He has made everything beautiful in its time. He has also set eternity in the human heart; yet no one can fathom what God has done from beginning to end.
ECCLESIASTES 3:11

Hope for the future stood me on my feet, and I got up from the depression at the turn in the road. I brushed the dirty leaves off my pants and continued to where the diverted trail rejoined the sunny path again. How happy I was to see the full sun and run along the path again! Sure, there would be bumps, scrapes, and more surprises, but I had emptied my pockets of the pebbles weighing me down and put the treasure of hope in their place.

The cabin. A quiet place to get away from the cares of this world.

10

Open, Sunny Path

And my God will meet all your needs according to the riches of his glory in Christ Jesus.
PHILIPPIANS 4:19

Walking a New Way
• • • • • • • • • • • • • • • •

I left the depression behind me and ascended a steep trail to the open, sunny path. When I stepped out into the sunlight, I realized that something was different. I looked around and then realized that it was me. I was different. I had a new identity. What made me Jeanie was not nursing, motherhood, JP+, farming, going to church, helping with the Gideons, or even Lee.

My identity was in being a follower of Jesus and a child of the Father. I began to practice walking in the Spirit, serving him, knowing that what I did mattered, but it didn't define me. This new reality created in me a momentum and free-dom to live life in a new way.

I began to break free of some of the pressure of perfor-mance. Sure, I still had patterns and habits around getting things right, being on time, and doing excellent work, but God was showing me that those were not the most import-ant things to focus on.

I am so glad that I decided to really throw myself into my JP+ business even after that difficult time when I thought I couldn't continue. God blessed that decision.

When I became a National Marketing Director in 2001, I was able to capitalize on the benefit package of the com-pany, which was remarkable—major medical, dental, health, and bonuses.

As the JP+ business continued to grow, so did our finan-cial health. We had never been in such a stable place before or had the flexibility we began to enjoy. Life became less about making ends meet and more about being proactive about our health, our relationships, and our activities. We also loved the freedom to give generously in a way we never were able to before. God had brought us from a place of receiving gifts of food and money to being able to give those things to others.

Coming Home to the Farm

By this time, the sadness of losing the farm was fading into the past. The pangs of defeat after fighting so hard to stay on the land were coming farther and farther apart.

We were content. God had showed himself faithful in each life stage and through each loss and blessing. Still, Lee would occasionally wistfully look over the auction pages, not even thinking the farm would come up for sale some-day. Then one day it did. He spotted it in a tiny ad in Decem-ber 2007, over 20 years after we had to leave. Lee looked up from the ad and said to me, "This is the home place."

We started thinking about whether we should try to buy it, but the questions were numerous. How could we? Should we even consider it? We were already in our early 60s. We asked each other, "Why do we want to go broke twice?" The auction was three weeks away.

We started praying.

Then Lee talked to Joe, a man at church, who owned and rented land close by the farm. In the course of the conversation Joe said that he had been approached six months earlier about buying it but it was priced too high. I simply stated that I would be happy with a few acres with timber and the pond.

Then while we were in Minnesota visiting Heather, Lee was really struggling with wanting to buy the land. He prayed, "God, I really want it, but I don't need it." Finally, he surrendered his desire to God and decided, "I don't have to have it."

The auction was the next Monday morning. Lee went to see old neighbors in The Hayloft where the auction was held in Grant. Joe was there and he and Lee sat down and talked about the land again. We were both interested in how it would sell. As the auction progressed it was not bringing near what we thought it would. When the auctioneer paused to take a break, Joe leaned over and said to Lee, "Are you interested in this land at this price?" To which he replied, "Yes." Joe said, "So am I. If we bought it, could I rent the pastureland?" Long story short, we bought it and divided it. Lee and I got 113 acres and Joe 103 acres. We paid $100,000 less than what the owner asked six months earlier. God was opening a door.

I knew Lee had gone to the auction, but I did not expect him to buy anything. When he walked in the door, I could see it in his face. I said, "You didn't. You didn't buy that, did you?" I couldn't believe it. After he explained to me the discussion between he and Joe and the price for the land, my shock suddenly turned to excitement, and I blurted out

"Can we build a cabin on it?"

Lee calls it a God thing. I would never have noticed the small ad, but he did, and after he surrendered his desire to God, things fell into place.

We began to realize that God was paving the way for something special to happen through our return to the family farm and building this cabin. God intervened, showing us that he was providing for every resource we needed to buy and build on the land. This included the road, electricity, water, and a fiberoptic line.

After buying the land, the next thing I knew, Lee was telling me that while he was up at the farm, he saw the road grater out working. He asked Lee, "Do you want a road up there?" "How much would it cost?" Lee asked. "Nothing," he told Lee, and it was done that afternoon.

Next God provided the electricity. The line had been slated to come out for three years but was never done. Lee told the electrical guy where he wanted the electrical line to go, and he didn't charge us anything for the work.

We needed a water supply. Lee remembered an old spring-fed cistern down by the pond that existed when his dad bought the farm back in 1961. Lee uncovered it, cleaned it out, trenched a line for a water pipe and power, and we had water. That became our fresh water source.

Not long before the foundation was poured, Lee saw a crew putting in fiberoptic cable around the corner out on the main road. He asked, "What would it take to run it up there?" They said, "Not anything now, but if you wait, it will be an arm and a leg." We needed the cable to go from where they were working up to where we were planning to build the cabin a mile on a dead-end road. "Give me a number to call," Lee said. After a few calls Lee met the project manager at the farm. "Usually, we run the cable up to a house," he told Lee. Turning around Lee pointed and told him, "Imagine a cabin right there." Lee's thought was it would be nice to have fiber optic, but we wouldn't be put out if we didn't get it. The manager said he would let him know. After not hearing from them for 3-4 weeks, they put the line in with no charge.

Then God enlarged the plan for the cabin. Initially, we were considering building a 24-by-30-foot cabin. Our oldest son said, "Dad, that's not big enough for the whole family!" Lee said, "It's not for the whole family, it's for mom and me." But then we started thinking how wonderful it would be to be able to host holidays with the 22 people we had in the family at that time. First Lee added 18 feet to the base cabin and planned for a loft to cover two-thirds of the main floor. Then we added a walk-out basement to the plan, and now we had a space that could host the entire family for Christmas. A few years ago, we added an attached garage and the "Blue Room."

In 2020, we, along with our son Chad, added another 295 acres adjacent to our farm. It's mostly timber, pasture, and ponds—wonderful for the grandkids to go camping, fishing, and hunting.

But family visits and celebrations are just a portion of the bigger plan God had in mind for bringing us back to the land we lost in the 1980s.

God placed a desire in us to share the farm to touch people's lives. Since we built the cabin, we have been able to share our home with many people. There have been several men's retreats and women's retreats at the cabin. Our son Chad has had business meetings with his team. Lee and I have hosted JP+ and Gideons' meetings there. Several couples and families have spent time there just to get away.

It has been our family's honor to host several Fourth of July parties for the community. The kids and adults play games, people brought what they wanted to be grilled, had great fellowship, and launched fireworks over the pond to mark the passing of another year of freedom.

It gives us such joy to be able to share with others what God has blessed us with.

Lee has done so much work around the place, including building the cabin, garage, and machine shed. We love to incorporate our kids and grandkids in the work and maintenance. While we work on projects, we have had such wonderful conversations with them. Outside, they have learned how to build buildings, fix fences, and cut weeds. Inside, the family has helped me clean the cabin, decorate for the seasons, and cook meals together. I especially love when they stay overnight, and we read from the *Blessing Book* and pray together. In doing so many things together, we have developed great relationships and they have developed a wonderful work ethic.

We really feel like we belong here along Williams Creek. It's hard to believe that even before Lee's family bought the farm, the creek already bore the family name. We've named our farm "Williams Creek Farm." Coincidence? Perhaps, but fitting for sure.

We walked that open, sunny path for what seemed like a long time. It was a path of blessing, challenges, and growth. Our faith muscles got strong, putting into practice the lessons we learned earlier in our life and marriage. We met many people along the road and helped as we knew we could. Then the path curved around to a land full of timber and a pond.

Our path had circled around to the farm we had lost in the farming crisis, and now it was returned to us. Today a cabin stands on the land as a reminder of God's faithfulness.

Part Three, God Blesses

11

Beyond Dreaming

But he said to me, "My grace is sufficient for you, for my power is made perfect in weakness." Therefore I will boast all the more gladly about my weaknesses, so that Christ's power may rest on me. That is why, for Christ's sake, I delight in weaknesses, in insults, in hardships, in persecutions, in difficulties. For when I am weak, then I am strong.
2 Corinthians 12:9-10

The deck at our cabin on the farm has a beautiful view of a large timber and the pond where the kids and grandkids like to play. When the weather cooperates, I sit here with Lee, sharing my heart and hearing his. Other times, I pray or sit quietly alone waiting to find out if Jesus has something to share with me.

To say living here is a dream come true is not accurate. I never would have dreamed of a blessing like this. But God did. Sometimes he blesses us beyond what we can dream.

From this spot I can see Lee walk out to the dirt garden or to the field to mend a fence or head around front to take care of the horses. I like to watch Lee work. We're both hard workers, and I'm blessed to have him as my partner and "buddy." Jay Martin, JP+ founder, always encourages Partners to "get a buddy" in their JP+ business, and Lee and I have always been that for each other in JP+, but even more, in life.

Lee and I have been walking life's path together for over 50 years! As I've described, it hasn't been a walk in the park, but a challenging hiking path! Financially and emotionally, we have enjoyed the ups and endured the downs. I am so grateful that we learned how to encourage each other in the droughts and floods of life. We have also learned to seize the joys in life when God provides them. I love these verses:

I know what it is to be in need, and I know what it is to have plenty. I have learned the secret of being content in any and every situation, whether well fed or hungry, whether living in plenty or in want. I can do all this through him who gives me strength. Philippians 4:12-13

"In plenty and in want" is reality in our case. We had to say goodbye to this dear farm and were blessed to return. Sitting on the deck reminds me of how faithful God is, and that knowledge helps me to pray in confidence to a good and loving God who put us together.

It's hard to believe our partnership started over 50 years ago near our cabin, when Lee asked me to marry him. Together, we've helped each other finish school, raise children, work jobs, move houses, build friendships, develop businesses, attend church and volunteer. We've done so many things together, as a team, using the unique gifts God gave to each of us.

Lee and I are very different from each other, which makes a great opportunity for growth and for filling in each other's gaps. One example of this is when we supported and watched each other become National Marketing Directors with JP+, both using our own unique skills to accomplish the same goal.

We are good for each other, as it says in Proverbs:
As iron sharpens iron,
so one person sharpens another.
PROVERBS 27:17

Blessed to be a Blessing
• • • • • • • • • • • • • • • • • • • •

Lee and I haven't walked the path we have for no reason! So many people who we care about have struggles. Many times, the struggles Lee and I have gone through apply to what another person is experiencing. It's a blessing for them to know they're not alone.

When JP+ entered our world at the second difficult financial time in our lives, we had no idea this new opportunity would give us the ability to be financially stable again, buy back the family farm, and be generous to others far beyond our imaginations. We would never have thought we could affect people's lives financially, supporting and mentoring them so they can begin their own journeys to healthy living in all areas of their lives.

I am so thankful that I said "yes" to the blessings of JP+. Through this journey, God has provided for my growth, friendship, finances, flexibility, the ability to give generously, and an outlet to use my gifts. It makes my heart full to think about.

For the first time in our lives, we are completely debt free! We no longer serve the master of the bank, and we are finally in a place where we can say that all our debts are paid. We are just so thankful that God brought us to this special place of financial health.

Recently Lee and I were at a JP+ Boot Camp. Lee was sitting in his work shirt with his arm over my shoulders and a young couple and young women came to tell us how we had impacted them over the years. Times like that remind me that I can only see a glimpse of how God may be using me where he has me.

I don't think I have any idea of what he might be doing through us by us just going about our daily routine and following what we think he is asking us to do.

A couple of years ago, I said to our accountant about the financial blessings we have had after all the hardship we endured, "I just feel like I don't deserve it." What he said surprised me. "You don't deserve it, but God has blessed you with it because you use it well."

Lee and I have talked a lot about that since then and we have come to say, "We are blessed to be a blessing."

It's easy to think in terms of people deserving what they get—or not deserving it. In advertising I hear a lot of messages about how people deserve things. It's a real temptation to justify other people's suffering or success in terms of whether their actions or efforts are deserving of their circumstances or not.

But God doesn't work that way. His grace and love go beyond an eye for an eye. I deserve nothing, but he gives me everything of true value!

Through the financial blessings God has allowed, we have been able to be generous far beyond what I ever imagined we would be able to give! Who would have thought, looking at our third ruined crop that bad year in the 80s, that someday we would be able to give to others?

My health struggles are another area that allows me to be a blessing to others who are struggling in their own bodies. I remember those times while working as a nurse and having MS symptoms while also building my JP+ business. God showed me in tangible ways how he is strong in my weakness. That is why I love those verses in 2 Corinthians 12. Sharing my story can encourage others that God can give them the strength to endure what they are experiencing.

Yes, God had made me a strong person, gave me parents who raised me to have a strong work ethic, and allowed me to develop a drive for hard work. But all of that could not overcome the weakness of my body or even the discouragement of my mind when I could no longer function on my own. There was no way I could function in my own strength. But God was faithful.

God showed me in a very personal way how to rely on him for the strength to function. When I realized that who I am is not tied to the things I do, I could rest in God's capable and powerful hands.

And God's power does not run out! When I began to learn to rely on him for my day-to-day activities and commit those activities to him, the important things got done, and he supplied what I needed to be a blessing to others.

It's a privilege to share my story with others. Sometimes a JP+ Partner will invite me on a Zoom call to share how MS and now JP+ have affected my life and how God has been faithful. Through interacting with others around my story, I hope to inspire them on to healthy living and growing closer to Jesus.

Being a blessing is really the basic point of my drive to care for others. Whether through nursing, JP+, Gideons, church or sharing finances or the cabin, I want to see people thrive in life. I want them to be healthy in their body, social life, finances, and in their spirits.

In their bodies, I want people to have a strong nutritional foundation and keep learning to take better care of themselves. Socially, I want them to build strong and healthy relationships with friends and family. Financially, I long for people to have opportunities to provide for themselves while still having flexibility in their lives and for their families. And most importantly, spiritually, I would love to see everyone I interact with touched by the love of my Father God.

Yes, Lee and I are blessed to be a blessing!

Our family on a sleigh ride in December 2021 having so much fun being together.

In Contentment and Freedom

• •

Getting to a place of financial freedom in Lee's and my life is all to God's glory. He has blessed us so much. We truly have lived the marriage vows, "In plenty and in want..."

I love to remember how God was so faithful to us in the most practical of ways during Bible school. The cash in the mailbox or the person with surprise groceries left lasting impressions on Lee and me.

Now, debt free, things are a bit easier for us. Those hard times could have tempted us to hold onto every penny, afraid bad times would hit again. But God has worked a miracle of perspective in our minds and hearts that allows us to hold what we have with open hands.

Because of that perspective, I believe that if something happened with our finances and things changed, I could go back to being very frugal again. I don't think I could say that if we had given in to the temptation to see money as a source of happiness. It's a trap our culture sets for each one of us. But when we began to see money as a tool and not an end, we escaped that trap. We were then able to allow God to use our financial health as a blessing to others.

I love a little game Lee and I play with God. Sometimes there will be a financial need that crosses our path where we would like to help. We'll both pray about it and come up with a number without talking to each other. Then we'll ask each other, "What number do you have?" Sometimes I go first, sometimes Lee. Usually, the numbers we both share are in the same ballpark, and often it's the same number!

Earlier in our lives when there were opportunities to reach out financially, we often felt like, "I don't know if we can do this or not." Now we have plenty, and that fact is attributed to the grace of God and the JP+ business he helped us to develop.

Lee and I have gone from wanting to being blessed; physically, mentally, spiritually, financially, and in our work and careers. Our hope is for the people in whom we "inspire healthy living" to trust God and find contentment when they are "in want," and to enjoy freedom when they are "in plenty" in all the areas of their lives. Contentment, freedom, and health; those are things to celebrate!

Now it's our turn to be able to surprise people with financial blessings. We've been able to give to missions, to church, and individuals in ways we never thought we could. We helped one family who had to quarantine due to COVID-19 and were going to suffer financial hardship because of it. We also can help our grandchildren with college expenses.

It's not just financial support we can give. God in his mercy has allowed me health despite my MS, to an incredible degree. Yes, I have struggles, but God always provides the energy and stamina I need to do the things he calls me to. One of these joys is to visit many of the grandkids during their first year in college. We have had some wonderful connection times during these visits, and I hope we have been an encouragement to them as they step out on their own journeys.

A Full Life
• • • • • • • • • •

My life after retirement from nursing continues to be full—full of movement and full of people. I am determined to do all I can to keep my body active and to maintain all the strength that I can to reduce the inflammation and continue living an active life. During the beginning of my retirement from nursing, I kept my body moving by walking with my neighbor.

In the past and now, as I'm able, I enjoy walking, using the Nu-Step machine and going to the YMCA. For a very long time, I didn't have to use a walker, but now after several falls, I use my walker all the time which allows me to be more active without as much concern about injury.

I also work hard at eating healthily and using the JP+ products to give my body every chance to stay healthy so I can enjoy the life God has given me and continue investing in the people God puts in my life. Lee has always supported me in these efforts, and even joins me in many of my goals. He never wanted me to have to make separate meals for him and myself, and is willing to eat the way I need to eat to take care of myself.

While taking care of my MS, Lee had health challenges of his own. When he got prostate cancer in 2011, it was a wakeup call for both of us. We realized that Lee needed to be taking care of his body as much as I needed to take care of mine if we were going to make the most of the days God would provide to us. Although he had been eating healthily with me as a way to support me on my journey to stay well despite the MS, after his own experiences he began in earnest to take even better care of himself through diet, exercise, and using the JP+ products.

Relationships fill my life; relationships with family, JP+,

church, the community, and through the Gideons. We have travelled all over the country keeping in contact with JP+ friends we care about. We have so many connections that Lee and I have developed a huge number of family-like relationships with other JP+ Partners.

Being a grandparent is such a sweet gift, especially because after the MS diagnosis, I thought I might never be able to be an involved grandparent. Lee and I really desired to have a relationship with each grandchild, and we have been able to be involved and invest in each of their lives.

A dear couple told us about the wonderful trips they took with their grandchildren when the grandchildren were nine years old. After we heard what a wonderful opportunity it was for them to invest in their grandkids, we decided to do the same.

Customer and Partner care is one of my favorite parts of interacting with people around JP+. I love to see the people I work with arrive at the next level, whether that is in their physical health, financial health by growing their own business, or personal growth in building a new skill or overcoming a personal challenge. I'm so grateful that this is my work now. Three to five years into JP+ I realized that this was true home health care, rather than what I call home sick care.

My work through JP+ allows me to use the gift God built in me to care for people in a whole new way. Retirement from nursing provided more time to invest in people and allow my influence to go deeper as I had the time to ask questions and really listen.

Through phone, Zoom calls, or Voxer messages I can reach out to people, encourage them, compliment them, and touch base with them before they go to a special event. I especially love the first of the month because I can see how much income a Partner made the month before and rejoice over their growth.

A sweet surprise that came out of my JP+ business was developing closer relationships with my nieces when they also got involved with the company. Going to JP+ conferences, I have seen them twice a year or more in our travels. It feels good to connect with family again. All our lives, we have lived 1,000 miles apart.

We have developed marvelous relationships at our church. I love praise and worship time and challenges from the biblical messages. A big part of my involvement is building and investing in relationships within the ladies' group. I enjoy the time we spend praying for each other and encouraging Bible study and prayer among the group. I meet regularly with several ladies in small groups and individually.

My biggest joy is to see the people I interact with know the Lord. Giving out New Testaments with the Gideons allows me to see this transformation. Traveling with the Gideons grows my faith as I see God move. Once, a check-in attendant took a Testament in her hands and burst into tears after reading the back page, which explains how God loves us and wants us to accept his son Jesus. She said she was glad to be able to share it with her husband who was passing away with cancer. Times like that keep me encouraged to continue giving Testaments to hotel attendants, restaurant servers, and filling-station attendants.

I have valued hospitality all my adult life. Now with the blessings of the JP+ business I have been able to do this more freely. I often have lunch with friends or invite someone to the cabin. One Thanksgiving, when our children and grandchildren were getting together with their other families, Lee and I invited over several older single people to our cabin for Thanksgiving dinner. We had a wonderful time reminiscing and laughing together.

I don't know what is next on the path God has me on. I hope I'm ready for it. It's been an exciting trip so far. For now, I will enjoy my life which God has filled with all my favorite things; peace, relationships, activity, work, and love.

So grateful to be enjoying the cabin together.

12

Rocks and Gems

If I started life by collecting stones and pebbles that weighed me down, I spent the middle of my life releasing those rocks to God and experiencing the growing freedom from their heaviness. Most recently, God has been filling my pockets with precious gems of peace and joy, and the blessing of reaching out to others.

I wish I could have shared with my younger self some of the freedom I have now. I wonder if I were to meet my younger self for tea at my special place, The Sweet Joy Shoppe, what would I say to encourage myself to stay the course trusting Jesus? Let me give it a try.

To child Jeanie, I would put my hand on her head and tell her that God's love is real and always there.

To myself as a young girl I would say, "Obey your mother. Don't go out to that movie with your friend. You know she doesn't approve of movies."

I would say to Jeanie as a young mom, "Being neat and tidy is important, but don't try to be perfect. Be more intentional about creating good, positive memories that are lasting. Relax more. Rest more."

When I was newly diagnosed with MS I'd say, "Trust in God. There is hope in him. He has a plan, and that plan is for your good."

I'd remind her of Jeremiah 29:11

"For I know the plans I have for you," declares the Lord,
"plans to prosper you and not to harm you, plans to give you
hope and a future."

To nurse Jeanie struggling to work with a migraine, I'd encourage her with the old saying, "This too shall pass."

To an agitated Jeanie with imbalanced hormones I'd also say, "This too shall pass."

When I was frightened with Lee working long into the night with large machinery, I'd tell myself, "It is difficult not to worry, but you can pray. Lean on your God. He is in control. You and your husband are in his capable hands."

When I was a new JP+ Partner finding my footing, I'd encourage myself to stick with it; don't give up; don't quit; and follow the system.

To newly retired nurse Jeanie whose identity had been in her work, my reminder would be, "Your identity needs to be in Christ now and his plan for you. Don't dwell on the past but look forward to God's plan. Trust him."

I'd give her Romans 12:2 which says, "Do not conform to the pattern of this world, but be transformed by the renewing of your mind. Then you will be able to test and approve what God's will is—his good, pleasing and perfect will."

On difficult MS days, I am grateful that God is in control and that someday I will have a new body. On all other days I remind myself to enjoy life! Enjoy my family! Live each day to the fullest! Anticipate each day's walk with God.

The hymn that often sings in my head as I'm reading my Bible is, "Turn your eyes upon Jesus. Look full in his wonderful face, and the things of earth will grow strangely dim, in the light of his glory and grace."

Sharing Gems

• • • • • • • • • • • • •

These days my life is full of intention. Intentional movement and intentional communication.

The movement is different than it was for me earlier in life. When I was younger, I was faster and I covered more miles, but I wasn't at peace in my striving for outcomes and my idea of perfection.

Living with the limitations of MS has been an adjustment for someone with such a busy personality and after living a full and fast-paced life. I've gone through a process to be content with my new reality and grateful for the good things that come with this change. That doesn't mean that I don't pray for a miracle. I do. Every day I pray for a miracle in my body, but God is doing a work in my spirit, and I know that I will have a new body someday.

Growing in faith is sometimes a slow and tedious process. All these changes are ultimately to develop Christ's character in me. I think of Romans 8:29, "For those God foreknew he also predestined to be conformed to the image of his Son, that he might be the firstborn among many brothers and sisters."

I also have the promise in Philippians 1:6 that he will complete his work, "being confident of this, that he who began a good work in you will carry it on to completion until the day of Christ Jesus." How comforting to finally be able to rest in that knowledge.

Reflection is easier now than it was in years past. I can settle in mind and spirit and spend quality time with the Lord. I love to reflect on his Word and pray for people who come to mind as I sit on the deck of our cabin, overlooking the little pond by the timber out back.

I wish I could have carried this peace and freedom with me earlier in my journey, but I needed all the experiences along the way to teach me to trust the Lord in deeper and deeper ways. Now I can remember and see his hand in each stage of my life and am grateful for how God has grown me. When I meet with people, I love to share what God has taught me and to encourage people to look for God in their own journeys.

I'm still a work in progress, but God has shown me that my life experiences are about his plan, not about me. I've witnessed him at work in how I relate to people about my passion for JP+ and sharing my faith through the work of the Gideons.

When people come into my life who are struggling financially, I can share about how Lee and I went through the farm crises and lost everything, but knew our hope was still in God. He provided during that time and has blessed us since then through the JP+ business, getting back a portion of the farm, building the cabin, and being able to give generously to others.

I can also encourage people struggling with their health when I tell them my story of hope. I share about when I was first diagnosed with MS and imagined the worst. I truly anticipated the same decline and death I had seen in the MS patients that I cared for as a nurse. But that wasn't God's plan for me. He provided the wisdom and direction to care for my body naturally, and then provided JP+ as an aid to fulfill that plan. He blessed me with the ability to hold each of my grandchildren—something I didn't think would be possible. I've even be able to attend four of their weddings.

So often, just being present and doing what I need to do allows me to encourage people. One day I went to the Y like I often do, and there was someone from church there. In just 10 minutes we were able to talk about some very important things going on in their life.

Through my JP+ business, I've told my story of hope to countless people: one-on-one, over Zoom, in three-way calls, and in front of groups. I encourage people to have hope because I have experienced hope in the eternal Creator God and his love for me.

My desire is for everyone to be healthy in their bodies and their finances so that they would not struggle with physical disorders or financial strain. More than that, my heart is for everyone to hope in God because he is the author of hope, true peace, joy, and life. With that hope, we can weather whatever comes in our path. We don't have to fear what is over the next hill, in the dark grove of trees or out in the open field. We can rest in our journeys, release the rocks and pebbles weighing us down, and receive from our Father God the gems he has for us as we walk with him.

He ran with me through my childhood and college days, walked closely with me in my early marriage and difficult financial years, carried me through long hours of nursing and raising small children, sat with me during the days of a new MS diagnosis, retirement, and depression. When I got back onto the open path of working with church, Gideons, and JP+, he never stopped teaching me and began allowing me to invest even more deeply in the lives of others.

At this point in my journey, God has led Lee and me back to the family farm. It is a double blessing. As precious as it was to us in our early life, it is more precious now. With generations of memories and the knowledge that it was a gift straight from God, the farm brings us a deep joy.

Epilogue

From Jeanie

As I've said, Lee is my buddy. He really is my biggest fan. God has blessed me through Lee. We have grown in love and commitment in famine and plenty. Lee's strong knowledge and understanding of the Word of God and his ability to explain and help me to apply it to my life has been a life changing and consistent influence.

And though this book has my name on it, he has been invaluable in putting it together. We are a team after all, and this project has really been a conversation. Whether it's working the farm, raising kids, or building a business, we do things together. So, it's only fitting that I let him talk a bit as we wrap up the book.

A Husband's Admiration, Words from Lee

One of my favorite things in the world is to watch Jeanie, my wife and partner, grow. We've been together since we were so young, and I've gotten to see her in so many situations. Since we both started working with JP+, I've gotten even more opportunities to see her use her skills. I've been there when she's met with, cried with, encouraged, brainstormed, nudged, loved and enjoyed people on their journey to healthy living.

It's probably normal for a husband to admire his wife and enjoy watching her! I've gotten to watch her for 54 years now. From the time I used to kick the back of her chair in class to popping in and seeing her working in her office today, I love to see her working, playing and even resting. Just two nights ago (we are hibernating at the cabin during the COVID-19 lockdown) when I came to bed, she was already asleep. I was about to turn off my bedside light and happened to glance over and see her face with the comforter pulled up around her, I paused a moment, just gazed on that angel face. I am so blessed.

Jeanie has an incredible ability to focus on what is in front of her. Sometimes it is a to-do list or a plan she is working on, but most often it is a face in front of her. Her blue eyes intent on loving a person and really hearing their heart.

I admire how she continues to grow. Early on, Jeanie kept a space between her and other people. You got this sense that she was reticent and reserved. I've seen her grow past some of that to the place where she is more outgoing and able to express who she is.

My greatest joy as a husband has been to see her grow personally. When I reflect through the years and remember, I see her really blossoming as a rose. I met her as a young rose bud and have gotten to watch her bloom as she becomes more and more of who God made her to be.

I've seen her grow in communicating person-to-person and in groups. In business she's grown in making decisions and relating to people. She grew in caring physically for others in nursing and then in caring for their spirits, souls and lives as God opened opportunities to care for them in other ways—including mentoring, praying, and inspiring healthy living in their lives!

Over the years, I've gotten to witness that growth as we've raised our children and now invest in our grandchildren. In her work with JP+, she has opportunities to share what she has learned with others.

Recently she reached out to a lady who had three children—one with special needs. She has been able to help them through mentoring and with finances. With our past financial struggles, who would have thought that we would be able to help people in those ways? But that is exactly what God does. He can help us to grow.

I like to think that I've had a small part in helping her to grow by loving her well. We have had our challenges in life, but God has proven faithful. I think often of the verses in Ephesians 5 that talk about Jesus loving his bride, the church.

Ephesians 5:25-27 says,

"Husbands, love your wives, just as Christ loved the church and gave himself up for her to make her holy, cleansing[b] her by the washing with water through the word, and to present her to himself as a radiant church, without stain or wrinkle or any other blemish, but holy and blameless."

Someday when Jesus presents his bride, everything will be complete—a magnificent, beautiful picture. I see Jeanie and I as a small preview of that. She is my beautiful bride, and I want her to be complete and whole as a person.

Jeanie's Admirers

Words that describe Jeanie:

Driven, Hospitable, Servant, Loving, Joyful, Servant-hearted, Giving-spirited, Hardworking,

Determined, Caring-Encourager, Loving-hearted, Passionate, Positive Influence, Honest, Caring, Good Sense of Humor, and Steadfast

From Lee:

I'm not the only person who admires Jeanie. She may not be the type who loves to stand up on the stage, but this world is full of Jeanie's admirers. I thought I'd let you hear a bit about what some of them have to say about her and her impact on their lives.

The first person is Chad Williams, who is our oldest son. I see so much of Jeanie in him—in his ability to schedule, his strong value of time. Also, his mind, like Jeanie's, is very analytical and thoughtful. Chad has a unique way of planning and getting things done. Chad loves to research and figure things out. He also has a deep sense of integrity and honesty. He has a heart that desires to serve God and others.

He's followed the growth of Jeanie's JP+ work and encouraged her along the way. Being a businessperson, he knows the numbers and follows along with the impact she is having on people. He is such a fan of his mom!

Chad Williams, Jeanie's son

• •

Mom is driven. When she got MS, she really applied that drive to improving her own body and looking for alternative ways to help her health. She got out of her comfort zone. Then she did the hard work to change her eating habits.

Growing up, Mom worked outside the home. She and Dad worked it so that we were never home without one of them. That meant she worked nights, at the hospital or the nursing home. She did whatever she needed to make that happen—and it meant great personal sacrifice.

Her hard-working nature is summed up in my memory of her mowing the lawn at the house we call "The Knight Place." There was a huge lawn with a deep ditch, and we only had a push mower. I remember mom mowing the lawn with my brother on her hip.

All these years later, she still works hard. I've heard her say many times with JP+, "It's all about the follow-up." If it's on her calendar, she'll do everything it takes to get it done. If we're in the car, she always has the laptop or phone out and is contacting people. She uses her time wisely, but when you're with her, you feel like you're the only person that she is interacting with at the time.

She is truly a life-long learner. I love to watch her as a

71-year-old still learning. It's been fun since she's been in JP+ because we share business and motivational books and talk about them.

She is always growing. I remember before JP+, mom was always the behind-the-scenes person. She was not comfortable at all in front of people. It's kind of crazy to see how JP+ has changed her ability to talk to crowds of people. She's very structured when she speaks and prepares every word, but it doesn't feel like she's reading.

But she's even greater one-on-one. Dad describes what it's like when they go to JP+ events. It's like she's a rock star. You can't go five feet without hearing, "Oh Jeanie!" People just respect and love her.

And so do I. I learned a lot from her growing up. Of course, I learned etiquette and good manners at the table. I heard "Don't talk with your mouth full" a lot. That was part of her teaching me hospitality.

I remember when we lived in the town of LaVista, Nebraska, we were often hosting and having people over. The house had an open-door policy. Mom and Dad didn't smoke, but there was an ashtray available for the people who did. She went out of the way to make people comfortable.

The first thing she does when people come is to offer them something to eat. Food is a big deal to her. She does a good job of making people feel at home.

Mom is a servant. I remember the time I had a big research paper to write in high school. We didn't have a computer at home, but there was one at school. I had some of the paper written, but I was a slow typer. She, however, was a fast typer. The solution to getting the paper done on time was that mom came after hours with me to school to type the paper while I wrote the rest. That's how she is. She would do anything to help her kids.

From Lee:
• • • • • • • • • • •

Christy Cunningham is Jeanie's dear friend. She's a dairy-man's wife and businessperson who has known Jeanie for 20 years. They got to know each other at a Bible study and in the last several years, they have developed a real sense of appreciation and respect for each other as they pray and share together.

They share many things and appreciate their many differences. Christy is an extrovert. Jeanie is an introvert. They are both very organized, scheduled, and productive and really complement each other even in their differences.

Christy Cunningham, Jeanie's friend
• •

I met Jeanie through our church, GracePoint Church. I've known her for 20 years, but recently I asked her if she would be interested in being my mentor. I found parenting my adult children difficult. So, for this next phase in my life I asked if Jeanie was interested in meeting with me to talk about life and family.

Jeanie is always so gracious and speaks quietly. She is generous, giving, and seems content, although I know that no one is always content.

I've watched her desire to fight this whole thing with her MS. She is not afraid to do the hard work to change her diet, do the exercises, and stay on a schedule. She is not one to just sit.

I admire how she digs into the research to find out what the disease is and then just stays diligent. She hasn't chosen the traditional medical route and she continues to study and learn and work with her body and trust that God is going to take her wherever He's going to take her.

Last year she was having trouble with her ability to move well. She had some fear of falling. I admired her tenacity and her willingness to share her walk with me and others. She is always trying to help other people by sharing her experiences—encouraging them to look at their options and treat their bodies well.

It's been a real encouragement to me to realize that I can do more than I've been doing. And I love that she's always in my court and is not afraid to say that I could be a little bit off.

I appreciate her faith and how she depends on God for things.

Through my meetings with Jeanie, I have grown a lot. I think I've stretched her a lot in her thinking too. I've seen more of an acceptance in her of her limitations as she continues to trust God. As we age, our trust levels have increased.

Jeanie's family is such a high value to her. It's so important to her to be a part of her grandchildren's lives. She has a deep love for Lee and a desire to support him in his Lincoln portrayals and travel with him. She wants to be there for her family and be a part of their lives.

When Jeanie and I meet we can both just be transparent with each other and share. She has a good sense of humor and a willingness to be herself.

From Lee:
• • • • • • • • • •

We met Sandy Arnold and her husband Scott through my cousin. Sandy is 10-12 years younger than we are, and also has MS and some health issues. Talking with her has been good opportunity to compare and learn from each other.

It's been an honor to be able to help her to grow her business and encourage her during difficult times. Jeanie and I and Sandy and Scott get along as couples. We sometimes meet at NMD [National Marketing Director] meetings and spend time planning together, doing calls together and praying for each other.

Sandy Arnold, Jeanie's soulmate

Jeanie and I met at a Juice Plus+ event over 20 years ago. We immediately had a kindred spirit kind of connection and shared a special bond through our faith. Soon, we started spending time outside of the Juice Plus+ community and developed a wonderful friendship.

I feel like Jeanie was placed in my life for a reason. One of our commonalities was a diagnosis of multiple sclerosis. Jeanie opened a door for me that gave me hope that I could take control of my diagnosis through lifestyle choices. I credit a lot to her regarding where my health is today because of her love and support. Over the years she became a beautiful mentor of mine not only in my health journey, but also spiritually and professionally.

When I think of Jeanie, I think of how very determined she is. She may have multiple sclerosis, but it doesn't have her. She does everything that her body will allow her to do. She leads a very full life despite her health challenges. I watch her defying the odds. Her positive mindset and staying so active over the years have been a life-giving influence to her and those she comes in contact with as she lives her life.

Jeanie is a prayer warrior! She is always so faithful in praying for others as she adds prayer requests to her prayer journal. I picture her doing her quiet time out on her deck at the cabin or at the condo in her comfy chair – praying to our Lord and Savior daily.

Jeanie is one who lives life to the fullest. When one looks at Jeanie, one doesn't see her struggles. A person sees her sparkling blue eyes and sincere smile. I feel very grateful and thankful for the relationship she and I have developed through the years. She has been a blessing to me in so many ways.

From Lee:
• • • • • • • • • • •

Heather is our daughter. When she steps into the room it is like sunshine that brightens the whole room, a breath of fresh air. She is insightful, loving and has such a serving, giving spirit. Heather is intentional like her mother. She gets things done and does so proficiently. She is honest and straight-forward in a very kind and gracious way. Heather's spiritual perception is remarkable.

Heather Whyte, Jeanie's daughter
• •

Mom is very servant-hearted, has such a giving spirit, and is extremely hardworking. I remember one time, probably when I was in middle school, when she heard about a family that was struggling and wouldn't have much of a Christmas. I think it was during the farming years, so we didn't have much ourselves, but Mom had us work together to put together a box with gifts and food. We took the box over to the family on Christmas Day and left it on their doorstep. I didn't even know who the family was. I love her giving heart, and this experience was one example that helped me to love giving to others as well. That attribute came from her.

Mom is very hardworking. She stayed up late and got up early to take care of our family, and she was always busy doing a variety of tasks. She worked very hard as a nurse while maintaining a huge garden and helping my dad with farming as much as possible. Her schedule varied, and at times she even worked nights as a nurse, but I don't ever remember her complaining.

She also modeled to me how to incorporate us kids into whatever she and Dad were doing, whether it was doing chores and work on the farm or cooking in the kitchen. I remember working together to can many, many quarts of green beans and freeze pints of peas. Once Mom found a recipe for fake pineapple that was made out of zucchini and since we had an abundance of zucchini, we canned quite a few jars and would use it in Jello! Without even knowing it, she taught me how to include my kids in daily tasks. I have seen friends who don't want their kids to be in the kitchen because they want things done in a certain way. Mom wasn't like that. She let us be messy and be kids! It became a natural thing for me to do with my kids, too. I am very grateful for all that Mom taught me growing up.

From Lee:

• • • • • • • • • •

Vanessa is our oldest granddaughter. She is loving, smart, fun-loving and humorous, athletic, driven like her grandmother and very disciplined. She entered college as a junior because of her high school college classes and graduated two years later with a double major. Jeanie and I call her our little CEO! She takes charge in a good way.

Vanessa Thompson, Jeanie's granddaughter

• •

I think of Grandma being at the cabin on the farm—her just standing at the door welcoming people into her home. She always loves having people around, feeding them, and loving on them.

Growing up, the highlight of the year was going down to Iowa for a week! Grandma and Grandpa would have us down in the summer for a week or 10 days. We would ride horses, bake in the kitchen, and help in the garden.

I remember being in the kitchen together and making things. Once, for Easter, we made a Bunny out of bread with dip and veggies. For Christmas, we made trees with broccoli and grape tomatoes, and peppers for lights.

I know that she's grown so much through her health journey. She's such a strong individual. She stays positive when it's a hard season. A lot of days she doesn't feel good. I just see her always go back to the Lord and stay positive on those days, and she continues to grow and be stronger when the times are harder.

Even physically, she continues to do a lot of things like physical therapy, going to the Y. MS is a thing that attacks your body physically. To go through that and keep on going is admirable. She has to treat her body carefully and do things to keep her body healthy.

Grandma has a lot of qualities to look up to and emulate. You can tell that every morning she is diligent in spending time with the Lord. Both grandparents take time to pray for us, friends, and JP+. I know they've carried that throughout their marriage. I want that for my life with my husband too, now that I'm married.

I love how encouraging and caring she is. She just has a big heart for people and wants to bring out the best in people and how they are living. It was super cool to watch how they were living their life together, as I was growing up. They influenced people's lives in a positive way by loving on them and encouraging them.

Grandma is super confident about JP+. You can see she wants to share her story and her journey with others so they can implement JP+ into their lives.

JP+ impacted me. I still take JP+ today. I do Shred 10 monthly with her. I try to eat super clean and be active. I love fitness and am into sports and being active. It's cool to do that alongside her as she does JP+

Growing up, for me, they had the gummies that I think are super fun for kids. Also, there were the Complete shakes. When I was in sports, I loved to make the shakes after working out. They are still a big part of my diet today. Healthwise, it really helped us stay healthy. I think it helped us get sick less, stay active, and do more with our bodies specifically.

From Lee:

• • • • • • • • • •

Brent is our youngest son. He is the father of a sweet family and loves the Lord. He works as a carpenter in Iowa about two hours from us. His carpentry skills are much better than mine. I have enjoyed working with him when the opportunity arises. He was a huge help with building the cabin. We have had many hunting experiences together. He loves the outdoors and is a true woodsman. Brent has grown so much spiritually and leads his family accordingly. Brent loves his mother so much and always asks "how is she doing?" and tells me to "give her my love."

Brent Williams, Jeanie's son

• •

Mom is caring, loving and steadfast, and she has definitely taught me how to give. She is a giver and values her family very much.

I really enjoy the phone calls I have with her and how she is proactive keeping in contact with me. When we are together, my favorite times are when mom's guard is let down, we get away from the business and are just able to be goofy and fun. I love being around her when she's tired because sometimes she gets giddy. At this point in my life, I look forward to the times when I feel like we're spending time together as friends.

She is very focused and intentional with what she does. She is committed and dedicated, working extremely hard—probably too much.

Mom is very faithful and steadfast in her work and cares very deeply. She really believes in what she's doing. That is why she's successful and why she's doing JP+. For her, it's about helping people because she's a helper. She is dedicated and caring with who she is in contact with. I think of her working in her office, loving to interact with people the way that she does. It brings her joy.

Her health journey has been very difficult for her at times. There have been times she's been defeated, but also times of victory. When she was first diagnosed, there were a lot of unknowns that lead to a lot of stress. We wondered "What is this?" and there were a lot of tests. Then once there was a diagnosis, she had a focus. She knew it was MS, and that gave her a determination and a focus to battle it and choose how she was going to do that. She became very determined to not just do her best to fight it, but to defeat it—and she hasn't succumbed to it.

I think that her health and JP+ journeys are intertwined. I don't think she'd have had her JP+ journey without her health issues. Being diagnosed with MS was the genesis of seeking first something that would help her and then sharing that with others.

Mom has grown in confidence in who she is, like being in front of people. I remember going to one of her first conferences and my dad being so proud and excited for me to see her speaking. I didn't know from being a child that this was a challenge for her, but I could tell through watching Dad looking at his wife speaking at that event that she was completely different.

From Lee:

Kayla is our granddaughter, our son Brent's daughter. I love Kayla's smile and laughter. Her blue eyes sparkle. She is reserved, however her love of Jesus shines. We have been horseback riding in the rain, and she has cooked with Grandma. A special time for us was her freshman year of college when we spent Thanksgiving with her in Montana.

Kayla Devalois, Jeanie's granddaughter

Grandma is honest, caring, and has a good sense of humor.

I love to watch her and Grandpa together and how they interact. They can be really funny, joking and making each other laugh as they talk together on the couch about stories from their lives.

She loves really well. I hope I can be like her someday—really generous, interested, not holding back, and wanting the best for people.

She is interested in my life, asking how things are going and praying for me. In high school, she was always supportive of the activities I was in and wanted to be there to show that she loved me. Even recently, she and Grandpa came out to see my husband and me and our new home together.

Being hospitable and making people comfortable are so important to her. Whether she is at the farm or the cabin, in the living room with everyone or in the kitchen, it's not ever a stressful time—it's always relaxed.

Grandma has been a godly woman to look to for a biblical marriage. I know that she loves her family and wants to provide what is needed. I look up to her for that.

She really loves the people she interacts with, works hard and wants to do the best she can. She has a huge heart for people and their relationships with the Lord, and also for their physical health. She puts those two things together. Since she's personally been affected by JP+ in a positive way, she uses that story to encourage others with or without health issues. She wants everyone to be healthy.

She has been important to my health and I'm healthier because of her and JP+. I don't remember a time without JP+ in it. When we were little, we weren't really aware of Grandma's health challenges. She really liked to be active with us. The only thing we knew was that loud sounds bothered her, and we tried to be quiet for her. She didn't want us to be burdened with her MS. But at the same time, we tried to be respectful and let her take her nap if she needed one.

Now it's harder for her to be active, but I never see her angry or upset about it. I think she's always just trusting the Lord, that he's taking care of her and will give her what she needs.

From Lee:

• • • • • • • • • • •

Josiah is our son Chad's son, the oldest of our grandchildren. Josiah is thoughtful and considerate. He is analytical and deep in his thinking. I love the way he cares for and encourages his siblings. He loves God and his wife deeply. He is giving Jeanie and me our first great grandchild.

Josiah Williams, Jeanie's grandson

• •

Grandma is caring and resilient with a quiet strength. She has influenced me through setting an example of hard work, not complaining in the midst of incredible pain, and through raising a family who loves the Lord.

She is a cheerful go-getter who loves to serve others. As a businessperson, she loves the people she gets to work with, and cares not just about them as coworkers, but also as people.

My favorite thing about knowing Grandma is her love for serving others and her care for those around her. When I picture Grandma, she is in the kitchen making healthy and tasty food for holiday meals, sweetly caring for those around her, and delighting in whatever her grandchildren are doing, whether playing piano, reading books, playing games, or whatever the activity of the moment is.

I love getting to hear stories about her childhood and hearing about how she would go sledding in the winter or would work on the farm with her dad.

It's been amazing to see how she has battled MS and still cared for those around her. She has not let the struggle of MS distract her from her relationship with God and others, and if anything, it has given her a strength and resilience that very few people have.

I'm blessed beyond measure to enjoy all my kids and grandkids.

End Matter

Suggested Resources

• • • • • • • • • • • • • • • • •

- *The 4:8 Principle: The Secret to a Joy-Filled Life* by Tommy Newberry
- *The Dream Giver* by Bruce Wilkinson
- *Leadership Smarts* by Ken Blanchard
- *Leadership by the Book* by Ken Blanchard, Bill Hybels and Phil Hodges
- *Bondage Breaker* by Neil Anderson
- *Living Behind the Mask* by Kay Arthur
- *Names of God* by Kay Arthur
- Any and all books by author Jim Rohn